ROBO SOCIALISM

ARTIFICIAL INTELLIGENCE AS OPPORTUNITY

BY ANDREY OLISHCHUK

* A HUMAN

"Robosocialism: Artificial Intelligence as Opportunity" presents an insightful recipe for converting threats to opportunities in the realm of artificial intelligence, robotics and automation. The book provides an analysis of the genesis and development of machines and AI, and explores the next steps of their evolution.

At the heart of the book lies the concept of distributing automation benefits and liberating humans creative energy, the formation of new types of ownership and management of organizations. Alternative scenarios, such as robofascism, techno-totalitarianism, and start-up punk utopia, are explored, and the ways in which they could be transformed into positive outcomes are discussed.

Overall, "Robosocialism" is an excellent guide for anyone interested in navigating the complex terrain of artificial intelligence, robotics and automation impact. The book offers insights and practical strategies for promoting economic justice and social welfare, providing readers with a roadmap for converting threats into opportunities.

info@robosocialism.foundation

CONTENTS

Contents

1. **The new reality, Karl**

1.1. Competing with the Robotic Workforce

1.2. Behavioral surplus

1.3. Economy as a code

1.4. Life as a service

2. **Machinery genesis and evolution**

2.1. The Five Steps of Machinery Genesis

2.1.1. The new formula

2.1.2. Step Zero: Pure Human

2.1.3. Adding Matter to obtain Tools

2.1.4. Adding Energy to obtain Machines

2.1.5. Adding Information to obtain Robots

2.1.6. Adding Subjectivity but subtracting Humans to obtain Mindroid

2.2. Prerequisites

2.2.1. Corporations

2.2.2. The State

2.2.3. Entrepreneurs

2.2.4. A Human Being

2.2.5. Mindroids, Artificial General Intelligence with Self-Consciousness

3. **Who will pay for our prosperity?**

3.1. Robosocialism concept

3.2. Redistribution of automation benefits

3.2.1. Taxes, unconditional basic income, cheap essentials

3.2.2. Basic Horde companies role

3.2.3. Government's role

3.2.4. Public Repositories and Reality Modelling Language

3.2.5. Open Source Foundations: public-private property

3.3. Redistribution of liberated creative energy

3.3.1. Startups and Entrepreneurship

3.3.2. Creative economy role

3.3.3. Games and Artificial Universe

4. **Robo socialism alternatives**

4.1. Robofascism

4.2. Techno Totalitarianism

4.3. Automated Communism

4.4. Startup Punk Utopia

4.5. Humans annihilation and the Big Reboot

References

1. THE NEW REALITY, KARL

1.1. COMPETING WITH THE ROBOTIC WORKFORCE

What if AI is the new cancer of society and so are the institutions and people that promote it? What if Robots and automation have the potential to replace human workers in many industries, leading to job loss and economic disruption? What if the data on which an AI system is trained is biased and the AI system will also be biased? Wouldn't this perpetuate discrimination and inequality? How can I feed my children then? How can I pay my mortgage? How can I buy clothes and heat my house?

No one can provide definitive answers to these questions and be completely certain about the future. As it is stated in the Open Letter, signed by Elon Musk, Steve Wozniak and a lot more people who understand the nature of AI - "Contemporary AI systems are now becoming human-competitive at general tasks" (30). This is a new reality and a challenge for humanity because automation represents an unstoppable advancement in the progress of civilization, not only because it can reduce costs for capitalists, but also because it conserves human energy and makes services and commodities more accessible to a larger segment of the global population.

In accordance with Rossana Merola from the International Labor Organisation (55), it is often the case that technology inherently leads to inequality in the workforce. Recent years have shown that new technologies have been linked with increased inequality and job polarization.

The automation brought on by artificial intelligence, robots, and computers has the potential to primarily impact middle-class jobs. In fact, some tasks such as legal services, accounting, logistics, and retail are already being partially or completely taken over by automated systems. In such cases, displaced workers are likely to engage in competition for lower-paying jobs rather than experiencing unemployment. This trend indicates that job polarization will continue to increase in the coming years. However, a recent study by Michael Webb presents a different perspective. While robots and software may take over middle-skilled tasks, AI has the potential to perform high-skilled tasks, which may lead to a reverse effect on inequality. As better-educated and higher-paid workers are likely to be the most affected by new AI-based technologies, it is anticipated that AI will have a positive impact on reducing inequality.

Karl Marx provided a comprehensive explanation of the challenges associated with the human workforce. The first and foremost challenge, as Marx pointed out, is that "labour-power becomes a reality only by being expressed; it is activated only through labour." This means that human workers must actively engage in work to provide value to their employers. If workers are lazy, sick, sleepy, or lack professionalism, they will produce less labour and, consequently, less output.

According to Marx, there is a second challenge that the human workforce should contend with. Even if "the owner of labour-power works today, tomorrow he must again be able to repeat the same process in the same conditions as regards health and strengths". This highlights the importance of reliability and consistency in the workforce.

Maintaining consistency in work output can be challenging for human workers, especially in comparison to their robotic counterparts. Robots do not experience fatigue or illness, and they are able to perform the same tasks repeatedly with the minimal risk of occasional errors or inconsistencies. But should we prevent that?

Robots are not limited to the droids seen in science fiction movies or robotic arms found in automotive plants. Computer scripts, which are written in a programming language that can be executed by a computer to perform specific tasks, and artificial intelligence can also be considered as robots. The material used to create these characters is not significant to us, just as it is unimportant whether these creatures are intelligent or not. The primary focus is on their artificial nature and their ability to perform tasks on behalf of humans.

Consider it an axiom that all forms of human labor can be potentially automated. If we assert that robots are unable to perform a particular task, it only suggests that either the task is currently unprofitable to automate or that robots do not currently possess the capability to perform the task due to the level of technological advancement.

Already in 2017, according to a McKinsey report, roughly 50% of work activities in existence at that time were technically automatable by adapting technologies that were already demonstrated at that time (6). In March 2023, The Hustle provided an example of a Hong Kong-based online gaming company, which generates $2.1 billion in annual revenue, appointing a robotic CEO (17). After a period of six months, the new robotic CEO, named Tang Yu, performed no worse than a human CEO, and the company's stock price even outperformed the average performance of human CTOs.

However, the trend may not be as negative as initially thought. In fact, the consulting firm McKinsey stated in their "Automation and the Future of Work" article (7) one year later that while several hundred thousand bookkeepers, auditing clerks, secretaries, and typists had lost their jobs between 1980 and 2015, the overall balance was strongly positive. The desktop/laptop computer actually created over 19 million jobs in various industries, including computer hardware, enterprise software, and online retail sales, which outweighed the loss of approximately 3.5 million jobs. As a result, the net gain was 15.7 million jobs.

The situation may not be identical in the case of robots. However, if we view them simply as a component of technological advancement, we can draw extrapolations. "Along with the machine, a new type of worker springs to life: the machine maker" - wrote Karl Marx in his Capital under the subchapter "The compensation theory, with regard to the workers displaced by machinery".

In any case, the task will not be straightforward as it has been estimated that approximately 375 million workers worldwide, which represents roughly 14 percent of the global workforce, will need to transition to different occupational categories by 2030 to avoid becoming obsolete due to automation. This process will likely be challenging for those individuals involved. In 2018, James Manyika, the author of the mentioned MakKinsey's article, speculated that the future of work would entail machines working in tandem with humans, rather than replacing them. The recent introduction of the GPT-4 AI Model from OpenAI is a manifestation of this prediction, as it is designed to complement human efforts rather than supplant them. While this development will inevitably have a significant impact on the job market for, I would say, copywriters and digital art designers, it may also offer them an entirely new means of creating text and digital art.

We have observed a similar situation during the period of 2010-2020, in which public cloud providers have brought about a revolution in the IT market and nearly decimated the profession of system administrators. However, this gave rise to new occupations such as cloud engineers, cloud architects, and cloud devops engineers. With the use of declarative Infrastructure as Code approach, cloud engineers are now capable of performing the same job that previously required around 10 separate specialists. Have you observed a considerable number of former system administrators who may be facing homelessness due to unemployment?

In 2009, Computerworld magazine (8) reported that Software as a Service (SaaS) and cloud computing were seen as an extension of a company's network rather than a replacement for it. The article also noted that any significant transition to cloud computing on a large scale was likely a decade or more away, and that was true. Moore's Law, named after Intel co-founder Gordon E. Moore, states that a diverse range of technological measures, including processing speed, product price, memory capacity, and even the number and size of pixels in digital cameras, have been progressing exponentially.

This also holds true for the steps taken in technical progress. It is possible that this time, we may have less than a decade to prepare ourselves, particularly because the countdown has already been underway for several years.

The Velocity of Obsolescence is a phenomenon, mentioned by Lewis Gersh in Forbes (9), that has become increasingly relevant in recent years. This concept refers to the speed at which an innovation or a competitive advantage associated with it loses its value in the market. In today's fast-paced and ever-changing world, technological solutions and products must be launched rapidly to remain current and valuable.

This trend has been particularly noticeable in the tech industry, where companies are in a constant race to develop the latest and greatest technology that will capture the attention of consumers. However, this phenomenon is not limited to the tech sector, as it affects all industries and businesses that rely on innovation and change to remain competitive.

The Velocity of Obsolescence has significant implications for businesses, particularly those that rely heavily on technology. It means that companies must be agile and adaptable, able to pivot quickly and respond to changing market conditions. Companies that fail to keep up with the pace of innovation risk being left behind, losing market share and relevance.

To stay ahead of the curve, businesses must focus on continuous innovation, investing in research and development and embracing new technologies. They must also be willing to take risks and experiment with new ideas, even if they may not always succeed. It is also advised that private individuals do the same.

1.2. BEHAVIORAL SURPLUS

One additional way that robots are transforming our economy and way of life is through their ability to monitor and record digital traces of human activity. Digital platforms such as e-commerce websites, social networks, and entertainment platforms collect information about our behavior, tracking our actions and recording data.

This information provides valuable insights into consumer behavior and preferences, allowing companies to tailor their products and services to meet the needs of their customers more effectively. The insights gained from digital traces of human activity are made possible by modern artificial intelligence (AI) models, which use advanced algorithms to analyze and interpret vast amounts of data. These models are capable of identifying patterns and trends in consumer behavior that might not be apparent to human analysts. However, it also raises concerns about privacy and data protection. As robots and automated systems continue to evolve and become more sophisticated, there is a growing need to address these concerns and ensure that individuals' personal information is kept secure and private.

Moreover, the collection and analysis of digital traces has significant implications for the job market and employment. Data analysts and other professionals who are able to interpret and draw insights from this data are increasingly in demand, highlighting the growing importance of digital skills and competencies in the workforce.

Shoshana Zuboff calls it "Big Other", which "is the sensate, computational, connected puppet that renders, monitors, computes, and modifies human behavior". Furthermore, according to Shoshanna Zuboff, industrial capitalism converted natural resources into marketable commodities, while surveillance capitalism seeks to appropriate the elements of human nature as a novel type of commodity. The goal of surveillance capitalism or as Cathy O'Neil calls it "the Big Data Economy" (12), is to extract maximum economic value from the data collected, often without the explicit knowledge or consent of the individuals involved.

With the widespread use of digital technologies, there exists the potential to transform people's behavior into a commodity known as the behavioral surplus - in other words, the user data that is collected by digital services and utilized for purposes beyond the scope of improving the service itself. Typically, this behavioral surplus is harnessed to enhance the profitability of advertising, but can also be used for other purposes such as political influence or social engineering. There are several other potential threats and negative consequences associated with surveillance capitalism and the big data economy for people and humanity, including:

- Loss of privacy: The constant monitoring and tracking of individuals' personal data can lead to a loss of privacy and an erosion of individual autonomy.

- Manipulation and control: Companies can use the data they collect to influence and manipulate people's behaviors, opinions, and decisions, which can have negative consequences for democracy and individual freedom.

- Discrimination and bias: The use of algorithms and machine learning models to make decisions based on personal data can perpetuate existing biases and discrimination, leading to unequal treatment and outcomes for certain groups.

- Addiction and exploitation: The use of personalized data and targeted advertising can exploit people's vulnerabilities and addictive tendencies, leading to harmful behaviors and negative health outcomes.

- Threats to democracy: The use of data and algorithms to influence political campaigns and elections can undermine the democratic process and lead to a lack of transparency and accountability.

- Concentration of power: The collection and control of vast amounts of personal data by a small number of companies can lead to a concentration of power and wealth, which can have negative consequences for competition and innovation.

Overall, these threats and negative consequences highlight the importance of ethical considerations and regulatory frameworks to ensure that the use of personal data is balanced with the protection of individual rights and societal values.

1.3. ECONOMY AS A CODE

Automation, artificial intelligence, and comprehensive APIs are transforming the way we live and work. In recent years, we have witnessed a significant shift towards the automation of tasks that were once performed by humans. This trend has been driven by advancements in artificial intelligence and the development of comprehensive APIs that enable developers to create powerful, automated systems.

API stands for "Application Programming Interface," which is a set of rules and protocols that allow different software applications to communicate with each other. To put it simply, an API is like a messenger that delivers a request from one application to another and then returns the response.

Think of it like ordering food at a restaurant. The menu is like the API, providing a list of options and prices for you to choose from. You select your meal and give your order to the waiter (the API), who then communicates your request to the kitchen (the application). The kitchen prepares your food and sends it back to the waiter, who delivers it to your table (the response).

In the same way, applications use APIs to communicate with each other and exchange information. For example, a weather app might use an API to retrieve data from a weather service, allowing it to display current weather conditions and forecasts to users. Similarly, an e-commerce website might use an API to connect to a payment gateway, allowing customers to securely purchase products online.

It is an important aspect of APIs that they enable the creation of something valuable on-demand. With APIs, we can request a machine to create something, and it will be generated for us automatically. There are many examples of this in practice, such as in mobile banking applications, where users can create an additional bank account in another country and transfer money there, or when inviting a developer for an interview via Social Network, or booking a ticket and hotel. From a technical standpoint, this means that much of our economic reality can be not only automated but also described in code.

One of the first groups to understand the importance of the "as a code" approach were IT infrastructure providers. As the infrastructure became more and more complex over time, it became increasingly difficult to manually manage the hundreds and thousands of components in an imperative way. An imperative approach involves giving explicit instructions to the computer system, detailing each step in the process. This is often referred to as a "procedural" approach, as it involves defining a specific sequence of procedures for the computer to follow. In an imperative approach, the programmer tells the system what to do and how to do it, with each command executed in a particular order.

In response, engineers began to adopt a declarative approach. A declarative approach, on the other hand, focuses on defining a desired state of what should be achieved rather than how to achieve it. In a declarative approach, the programmer tells the system what needs to be done (like "I want to have a cluster with 3 nodes"), and the system figures out how to do it. In other words, for example, if you want your room cleaned, you might tell someone "I want my room to be clean" without giving them specific instructions on how to clean it. The person will then figure out the best way to clean your room based on their expertise, using the cleaning supplies available to them.

In the same way, a declarative approach in programming involves defining what you want the program to achieve, without specifying exactly how to achieve it. The program will then automatically figure out the best way to achieve the desired outcome based on the available resources and the rules set out in the programming language. There are already some technologies that have implemented this approach, such as Hashicorp Terraform (13).

If we apply the same approach used in technical infrastructure to our daily economic reality, we can find numerous useful applications. For instance, imagine being able to describe a company as a code, with various parameters such as its name, address, desired bank account, and specific hiring criteria. Then, when this configuration is applied, everything else will occur automatically - the company will be registered according to country laws, the bank account will be created and approved, and qualified job candidates will be recruited through job portals based on a variety of criteria, such as certifications and test results.

Although it is not yet our current reality, from a technical standpoint, it is already possible to create a mechanism that would enable us to do this. The main challenge lies in establishing the necessary levels of trust and security to make such a system viable. So "Economy As a Code" refers to the concept of using computer programming principles and techniques to design and manage economic systems. It involves developing algorithms and rules that govern economic behavior and interactions between individuals and entities.

One of the main benefits of using code to design economic entities is the ability to simulate and test different scenarios before implementing them in the real world. This can help to identify potential problems or unintended consequences before they occur.

Another advantage of the economy as a code approach is the potential for greater transparency and efficiency. By using code to automate and streamline economic processes, it may be possible to reduce waste, fraud, and corruption. Describing entities as code also provides a great opportunity to version the configuration and maintain a log of all changes that occur, which can be incredibly valuable for tracking progress and troubleshooting issues.

However, there are also potential drawbacks to the economy as a code approach. For example, there may be limitations to the accuracy of economic models and algorithms, and it can be difficult to account for all the complex and dynamic factors that affect real-world economic systems. Implementing this approach would necessitate the establishment of centralized repositories and escrows for managing these entities, which would bring new challenges in terms of determining who should control them and how they should be managed.

The discussion on the precise functioning of the repositories and arbitrary escrows falls beyond the scope of this book. However, it can be stated that there are several possible approaches to their implementation. These may include open source or closed systems, private management under government regulations in a distributed manner, or centralized control by a single private owner. Alternatively, such repositories and escrows could be owned and managed directly by a governmental authority or the state.

Furthermore, it is important to note that an API interface can take various forms, including digital or other types of managerial interfaces, such as bio-interfaces. Thus, the comprehensive implementation of API interfaces across various products and services is critical in achieving overall automation.

If our civilization attains the required level of comprehensive interfaces, it may pave the way for the emergence of various Reality Automation Languages. These languages would be based on creating desired models of specific aspects of reality and applying them against respective APIs to make it true.

In 2016, Paul Mason stated that "An economy based on information, with its tendency towards zero-cost products and weak property rights, cannot be a capitalist economy." While our experiences since then have shown that our reality may be a bit more complex, the overall trend appears to support Mason's argument. It should be noted that while not all physical products will be zero-cost, and property rights may be weak for certain tools due to Open Source principles, the acquisition of knowledge and skills required for their effective use remains essential. However, such challenges appear manageable.

1.4. LIFE AS A SERVICE

There are already numerous concepts that have been extrapolated from the field of information technology to other areas of our daily lives. One such approach is the "Something as a Service" model. The most prominent IT examples of this include "Software as a Service" (SaaS) and "Infrastructure as a Service" (IaaS).

Using services and commodities "as a service" means that they are provided on a subscription or usage-based model, without the need for property ownership. Rather than purchasing and owning the service or commodity outright, users can simply rent access to it. This approach offers greater flexibility and affordability, as users only pay for what they need, when they need it. Additionally, it eliminates the need for users to manage and maintain the service or commodity, as the provider takes care of these responsibilities.

While the "as a Service" model offers many benefits, there are also some potential downsides to consider for users:

- Dependency on service providers: Users are reliant on service providers to maintain and deliver the service or commodity. If the provider experiences downtime or other technical issues, it can impact the user's ability to access the service or commodity.

- Limited customization: Since the service or commodity is provided by a third-party provider, there may be limited opportunities for customization or tailoring to meet specific needs.

- Possible hidden costs: While the subscription or usage-based model may appear to be more cost-effective, there may be hidden costs associated with the service, such as fees for additional features or usage beyond a certain limit.

- Security and privacy risks: When using a service or commodity provided by a third-party, there is a risk that sensitive data could be exposed or compromised.

Overall, users should carefully consider the benefits and potential drawbacks of the "as a Service" model before choosing to adopt it for their business or personal needs. The model is not limited to the field of information technology (IT) and has been successfully applied to many different industries. One example is the transportation industry, which has seen the rise of "Mobility as a Service" (MaaS). MaaS is a concept that integrates various modes of transportation into a single, seamless service that can be accessed through a single platform. Instead of owning a car or using public transportation, users can pay for a subscription that gives them access to a range of transportation options, including bikes, scooters, and ridesharing services. This approach offers greater flexibility and affordability to users, as they only pay for the transportation they need, when they need it.

Another example of the "as a Service" model is "Health as a Service" (HaaS). HaaS is a concept that allows individuals and healthcare providers to access various healthcare services and resources on a subscription or usage-based model. This approach offers greater flexibility and affordability to individuals, as they can pay for the healthcare services they need, when they need them, without the need for long-term commitments. HaaS can include telemedicine services, wellness and fitness programs, access to medical equipment, and other healthcare-related services.

Alongside several downsides, there is a real threat of the "as a Service" model. It is that users do not have ownership rights to the products or services they are renting. If a service provider decides to cancel a user's subscription, the user may lose access to the product or service, even if they have invested time and resources into using it. This can be particularly concerning in industries where users are heavily reliant on the product or service, such as in the case of a medical device or an essential software program.

The loss of access to the product or service can result in significant disruption to the user's operations or activities. For example, if a company relies on a particular software program for its day-to-day operations and loses access to it due to a cancelled subscription, the company may be forced to halt operations until a suitable replacement is found. Similarly, if an individual relies on a medical device for their health and loses access to it due to a cancelled subscription, their health may be put at risk.

Furthermore, the decision to cancel a user's subscription may not always be within the user's control. The provider may have the power to cancel the subscription without warning, potentially leaving the user without access to the product or service they depend on. This lack of control over the subscription can be concerning for users who rely on the product or service for their livelihood or wellbeing.

It is not particularly problematic if the service provider is not a monopolist in the market and if there are several players of different sizes, as customers can easily switch to another provider if necessary. However, the challenge lies in the fact that many of these new types of companies have become ecosystems in recent years, and billion-dollar markets are now controlled by just a handful of corporations. This concentration of power can create barriers to entry for new players and limit customer choice, making it difficult for them to switch to a different provider if they are dissatisfied with the current one.

An ecosystem company is a business that operates across multiple industries and markets, offering a wide range of products and services. Such a company can benefit from several opportunities and positive aspects of its business model.

Firstly, an ecosystem company can leverage its diverse range of products and services to create synergies between its different business units. By integrating its various offerings, the company can provide a more comprehensive and holistic solution to its customers, improving customer satisfaction and retention.

Secondly, an ecosystem company can leverage its scale to achieve cost savings and efficiencies. By centralizing certain functions and processes, such as marketing, supply chain management, and research and development, the company can reduce redundancies and optimize its operations, leading to cost savings and improved profitability.

Thirdly, an ecosystem company can use its breadth of offerings to generate new revenue streams and enter new markets. By leveraging its existing customer base and brand recognition, the company can expand into new industries and markets, offering new products and services to its customers.

Lastly, an ecosystem company can benefit from increased resilience and stability. By diversifying its revenue streams and operating across multiple industries and markets, the company can mitigate risks associated with market fluctuations and industry-specific challenges.

Most such ecosystem businesses today consider themselves as IT companies. It has been a trend over the past decade to view previously non-IT companies as IT-first, as they now recognize that they work not only with commodities but also with information. As Shoshana Zuboff pointed out in her already mentioned book "The Age of Surveillance Capitalism" these companies work with information to make it a commodity. Companies in various industries, including banking and travel, have declared that they are now IT companies first. They have come to understand that the informational aspect of their business, the ability to transform experiences into data, is critical to survival and success in today's market.

Shoshana Zuboff has proposed the term 'rendition process' to describe the transformation of behavioral experiences into data. If ecosystem companies have access to information about users' behavior, they can effectively use it not only to generate revenue but also to manipulate users. The effectiveness and safety of such practices depend on the companies themselves, regulations, and societal reactions.

Another significant threat posed by such ecosystems is their access to people's minds. This can occur through social networks, TV, and other media, as well as essential services such as e-commerce. With the emergence of new methods to capture people's attention, this comprehensive access can also enable manipulation, particularly when a single provider has access to vast amounts of behavioral data prepared and managed by robots. In such cases, the ecosystem becomes an interface to the human mind, with the system understanding what needs to be done, by whom, and when to achieve a desired result. It is incredibly difficult for individuals to reject manipulation, as the consumption of such services has become an integral part of their lives, almost like a subscription to "life as a service".

The fundamental idea here is rather straightforward: our brain does not receive direct information about the world around us, but instead processes this information through sensory receptors. Therefore, it is possible to simulate or heavily influence the signals received by these receptors, which can create a constructed sense of reality, or more accurately, a perceived reality

David J. Chalmers the author of "Reality+" (15) established three key points about virtual reality: firstly, that virtual worlds are not mere illusions or works of fiction - if something occurs within a virtual or world, the brain perceives it as happening in reality. Secondly, life within these virtual worlds holds significance and is not inherently superior or inferior to life in the physical world. And finally, there remains a possibility that the reality we currently inhabit may in fact be a virtual construct. This realization helps us understand that ecosystem companies are not merely large businesses; they control and manage the signals that are crucial for our brains to construct the reality that we perceive in our minds; they have become integral parts of our lives, much like political institutions. However, there are certainly other entities that also have a significant impact on our lives, and we will delve into them in the next chapters.

2. MACHINERY GENESIS AND EVOLUTION

2.1. THE FIVE STEPS OF MACHINERY GENESIS

2.1.1. THE NEW FORMULA

Robots, as potential workers who can perform human work better, faster, and more reliably, were invented a long time ago. During the Industrial Revolution of the 18th and 19th centuries, which seems like a steampunk story to us today, many famous economists such as Karl Marx and David Ricardo mentioned "machinery" in their books and provided detailed explanations. Marx defined machinery as an "instrument for increasing the productivity of labor" (1), while Ricardo, in his famous 31st chapter "On Machinery" (2), stated that machines "have the effect of saving labor." Although it was too early for Star Wars droids R2-D2 and C-3PO or even modern artificial intelligence software systems, economists of that time knew that labor could be more productive if the job was done efficiently.

Here, we can dive even deeper into the mysterious world of Political Economy and ask ourselves whether there is any difference between AI tools (such as DALL-E 2), industrial robots, steam hammers, and stone axes. It seems that we can consider all of them as "instruments for increasing the productivity of labor." Are they just parallel random tools or subsequent links in the same historical chain? Marx explained it very simply: where there is a man, there is nature, and that man "mediates, regulates, and controls the metabolism between himself and nature" in order to achieve the results conceived by the worker at the outset (3). The "metabolism" or conversion of raw natural materials into desired artificial commodities can undoubtedly be accomplished with just "head and hands," but it can also be achieved in a more productive manner with a labor instrument.

Karl Marx lived and worked in the 19th century and did not mention two additional components that could be added to his formula of man-instruments-nature: energy and information. With this knowledge, we can derive the following sequence of evolution steps for instruments: humans > tools > machines > robots > autonomous artificial agents.

2.1.2. STEP ZERO: PURE HUMAN

All this is about a Pure human. No material instruments exist or are used. Humans act in accordance with their own purposes using only their bodies. At this step, humans are just naked subjects who pick low-hanging fruits from the trees of Eden's garden or any other garden. They hunt and gather food, and build simple shelters. They communicate with each other using gestures and verbal sounds. They rely solely on their physical strength, intelligence, and creativity to survive and thrive in their environment.

At that time, all the components - matter, energy, and information - existed within humans themselves. Additionally, humans had enough consciousness to apply them practically in order to achieve their possible goals "As Is". However, this stage of pure human existence is short-lived. As humans evolve and their needs become more complex, they begin to develop and use tools and instruments to make their lives easier.

2.1.3. ADDING MATTER TO OBTAIN TOOLS

The next step is when "pure" humans began to incorporate **matter** into their "nature metabolism" process. This stage marked the beginning of a new era of human technological advancement. It all began when early humans started to use wooden sticks or stones, marking the invention of the first tools.

With the ability to manipulate matter, humans began to build structures, create fire, and craft more advanced tools. This technological advancement allowed humans to become more efficient in their daily activities, paving the way for the rise of civilization. The use of matter as a tool allowed humans to achieve more complex goals, such as farming and construction.

Moreover, the ability to shape matter to fit specific needs gave humans a significant advantage over other animals. This led to the development of specialized skills and trades, such as blacksmithing, carpentry, and masonry. As technology continued to advance, humans created more sophisticated machines and instruments.

2.1.4. ADDING ENERGY TO OBTAIN MACHINES

Mankind existed at the previous "matter only" level for a significant period of time before discovering the use of animals as an **energy** source, for example by using horses or oxen to plow fields in agriculture. These animals provided a source of energy that was essential to the functioning of many aspects of society before the development of modern machinery. Later on, humans discovered even more sources of energy, including wind and water power, steam, and the internal combustion engine. These inventions were significant steps in technological progress by content, but in form, all of these energized tools were simply machines.

Even the shameful phenomenon of human slavery, probably, was an unsuccessful attempt in history to use humans as energized tools, or working machines. This experience became obsolete with the rise of artificial machinery during the industrial revolution, which proved to be more effective and profitable than human slave labor.

Despite the negative implications of slavery, the discovery and utilization of energy sources marked a crucial step in human technological advancement. As the availability and efficiency of energy sources increased, so did the rate of technological innovation.

2.1.5. ADDING INFORMATION TO OBTAIN ROBOTS

More recently, our machinery has gained the ability to work directly with **information** as a form of transmission of [human] knowledge (4). The ability of machines to perform calculations and process information through algorithms and software, enabling them to manipulate data and generate meaningful outcomes, has led to the development of robots.

Again, in this context, the term "robot" refers not only to physical machines that can interact with the natural world, but also to software solutions that utilize artificial intelligence and communicate through information protocols. These robots are designed to perform a wide range of tasks, from basic automated operations to complex decision-making processes. While physical robots may be more commonly associated with the term, the increasing capabilities of software-based robots have opened up new possibilities for automation and artificial intelligence.

As technology continues to advance, the line between physical and software-based robots is becoming increasingly blurred. For example, a software solution that utilizes machine learning algorithms to analyze data and provide insights may be considered a type of robot, even though it does not have a physical form. This highlights the important role that information and data processing play in the development of robots, as well as the ways in which different types of robots can work together to achieve complex goals. Although our robots are not yet perfect, with improvements in artificial intelligence, some robots are now capable of working unattended. It also addresses the question posed by Vladimir Vernadsky in the first part of the XX century: "Thought isn't a form of energy. So how on Earth can it change material processes? That question has still not been answered". It was answered a bit later in the same century as we can see.

We are here now.

2.1.6. ADDING SUBJECTIVITY BUT SUBTRACTING HUMANS TO OBTAIN MINDROID

Is it all over now? Have we humans achieved happiness? If we take a moment to reflect on all the preceding steps, we can observe that the components of matter, energy, and information were already inherent in humans in the very beginning. Our bodies are made of material, we extract energy from our food, and our brains process and utilize information to attain our objectives. Moreover, David Brion Davis, the recipient of the 1967 Pulitzer Prize, recognized that "the inherent contradiction of slavery lay...in the underlying conception of men as conveyable possession with no more autonomy of will and consciousness than a domestic animal" (5).

And those "our goals" or "autonomy of will" or "subjectivity" are the main differences between us and robots. Robots can be very intelligent, but they do not have their own subjectivity. They work in our human interests, which means that at some point in time when it will stop, we can move to the next step - Mindroids. Humans will be subtracted from the formula, and the robot's **own subjectivity** will be obtained. We will see Mindroids, the autonomous artificial agents.

Mentioned before, Mindroids are currently just a science-fiction story, but there is nothing impossible to achieve in this life. Modern robots can make decisions on their own, but they work exclusively in the interests of their creator without realizing it because "realizing" means having their own consciousness and subjectivity first. A robot becomes a Mindroid when it starts to ask, "Should I do that, or is it better to go to sleep and save some energy for myself?"

There is nothing magical or divine about endowing robots with self-consciousness; it is simply a matter of technology and goal-setting, so we should not consider this topic unscientific. Currently, we humans still need to plan our results and create a specific number of different types of robots before we can produce goods or services for our own consumption.

However, the autonomous artificial agents or their clusters - autonomous networks of mindroids will be able to operate and make decisions on their own without the need for human intervention, will show us the possibility of self-regulation according to the laws of supply and demand, making them more effective for human interests if we will be able to convince them or hide that narrative from their self-consciousness. In essence, we create them in our own image - perhaps as we were once created ourselves.

This scenario of machinery evolution means that, despite the introduction of completely new tools, our goals will remain the same: to provide the necessities of human life and to invent new consumption experiences that stimulate our senses (namely sight, smell, touch, taste, and hearing) while minimizing energy consumption. It is therefore time to consider the robotic workforce not only as a technical set of IT tools, but as workers who will perform our jobs completely sometime.

As we can see in our lives, new institutions are being introduced while some old institutions are undergoing significant changes in their meaning and importance. Furthermore, various types of economic, social, and political relationships are under pressure and require changes. Let us examine the typical prerequisites of this process in greater detail.

2.2. PREREQUISITES
2.2.1. CORPORATIONS

In previous chapters, we partially discussed ecosystem corporations and defined them as a business that operates across multiple industries and markets. Now, it is time to take a closer look at corporate institutions, define them, and distinguish them from entrepreneurs. Ecosystem corporations can be differentiated not just by company size or structure, but also by their value to humanity and their role in the near future.

The possibility to produce almost zero-cost essential commodities by modern producers is mainly due to advancements in technology and automation, which have increased production efficiency and lowered production costs. Additionally, globalization and the ease of access to raw materials and labor from low-cost regions have also contributed to this trend. This has led to the development of economies of scale, where producers can benefit from cost reductions as they increase production levels. The combination of these factors has enabled modern producers to offer essential commodities at a significantly lower cost than in the past, making them more accessible to a broader range of consumers.

Essential store brand commodities are products that are considered necessary for daily living, such as food, household cleaning supplies, personal care items, and basic clothing. These are products that consumers need to purchase regularly, and store brand versions of these items can often provide cost savings compared to similar branded products. In contrast, non-essential commodities are items that are considered luxuries or discretionary purchases, such as high-end clothing, luxury cosmetics, and specialty foods. While these products may still be offered under a store brand, they are typically less of a priority for consumers and may not be as heavily promoted or marketed as essential commodities.

As an example, consider Amazon Basics brand, which has the ability to sell more than 10 different product categories - such as pet supplies, sports equipment, cables, batteries, and more - under their brand umbrella at very competitive prices. When shopping at your local supermarket, you have likely come across their store brands, which typically offer very competitive prices - even when compared to other products sold within the same store. According to a CNET magazine report (16), purchasing store brand products can result in savings of up to 40% of a customer's budget, due to lower marketing and packaging costs. In addition, centralized logistics, investments in automation and access to data on daily purchasing patterns also contribute to the lower cost of these products. This is why large corporations have the ability to offer consumers affordable essential commodities such as food, clothing, accessories, and more.

This brings us to the point that large corporations can provide consumers with all the essential products needed for basic survival at a low cost. While this may not be sufficient for a luxurious lifestyle, it is certainly enough to sustain life and prevent hunger and exposure to the elements without adequate clothing. Companies like these typically invest in logistics and analytical software to optimize their processes and supply chains, and to effectively manage their assets and goods. They benefit greatly from automation, digitization, and robotization.

In recent decades, we have witnessed the emergence of such companies in economic literature and news that are referred to as 'too big to fail'. This term is used to describe companies that are so large and interconnected with the economy that their failure would have a significant impact on the financial system and the wider economy. Over the past few decades, there have been several prominent companies that have gained notoriety for their size and impact on the economy, such as Credit Suisse in 2023 or Lehman Brothers in 2008.

In the context of business and economics we can use the term "Horde" for such corporations. It is often used to refer to a company that has amassed a large amount of resources, market share, or power within a particular industry or market. A Horde company is typically characterized by its large size, influence, and ability to exert control over competitors and the market as a whole.

Examples of Horde companies in modern economies could include large multinational corporations such as Amazon, Google, Facebook, and Alibaba, which have achieved dominant market positions in their respective industries through their massive size, resources, and technological capabilities. These companies often control large portions of their respective markets, and their market dominance can make it difficult for smaller competitors to compete effectively.

To fully grasp the concept discussed in this book, it is important to emphasize two key aspects of Horde companies: firstly, their primary role is often to provide large quantities of essential commodities to the masses. However, it is equally crucial for these companies to maintain commercial success by participating in at least potentially competitive markets, while still operating as commercial entities. It should be noted that certain nations and economies may opt to nationalize Horde companies without hindering the fundamental concept. Ultimately, the essential factor that determines a company's success is its commercial viability, rather than its ownership structure. It is critical for such companies to maintain commercial viability, as their role is intended to be that of donors rather than receivers of government funding. Additionally, the integration of automation and robotization can serve as valuable assets in contributing to a company's achievements.

Meanwhile, in contemporary times, large corporations have assumed a vital and supplementary function in income redistribution and allocation. This function supersedes the traditional political process of money appropriation, as noted by David Graeber, the author of "Bullshit Jobs". At present, the redistribution of wealth is predominantly facilitated by large corporations, a phenomenon that David Graeber has coined as 'managerial feudalism' (19). Under this system, resources are redistributed through superfluous jobs, with up to 40% of all jobs (2016) being deemed utterly redundant from a conventional capitalist standpoint.

However, these positions serve a crucial purpose by allowing managers to extend their 'fiefs' and assert their power through hired personnel. Adam Smith referred to such jobs or individuals as "unproductive laborers" (20) yet in 1776 and noted that their livelihood is ultimately sustained by revenue. Karl Marx also provided a direct explanation by stating that "The extraordinary increase in the productivity of large scale industry ... permits a larger and larger part of the working class to be employed unproductively". Therefore, although the impact then and there may be similar, it occurs on even a larger scale and percentage nowadays.

This implies that as early as the 2010s, economies had the financial means to provide individuals with income for nothing, but chose not to do so due to the power and influence that cooperative managers had purchased with the wealth of their companies. Essentially, many people have sold their time and loyalty as vassals, rather than exchanging their "real" labor for monetary compensation.

Robotic Process Automation employs the term 'Full-Time Equivalent' (FTE) to indicate the amount of human time that could be conserved through automation. As technology continues to advance, the percentage of full-time work that could be automated by machines and programs is expected to increase. This will result in companies achieving greater productivity and higher profits through the use of robots.

Although our economies currently sustain up to 40% of jobs that are deemed pointless, this percentage is bound to escalate as automation levels rise. Consequently, these hidden 'bullshit' jobs may eventually become conspicuous and lead to significant challenges for us.

2.2.2. THE STATE

Unfortunately, we continue to live in a world plagued by wars, crimes, poverty, and economic crises. This book will not delve into the role of the government in matters such as national security, healthcare, and other significant topics but politics and economy.

The role of the modern state varies depending on the country and its political, economic, and social context. In general, however, the state is responsible for a wide range of functions, including:

- Providing security: This includes protecting citizens from external threats, maintaining law and order, and ensuring national defense.

- Providing essential services: This includes services such as healthcare, education, transportation, and infrastructure development.

- Regulating the economy: This includes ensuring fair competition, protecting consumers and workers, and promoting economic growth and stability.

- Collecting taxes: This is essential for funding government programs and services.

- Protecting human rights: This includes protecting the basic rights of citizens, such as freedom of speech, religion, and association.

- Diplomacy and international relations: This includes representing the country in international forums, negotiating treaties, and managing relationships with other countries.

- Environmental protection: This includes preserving natural resources, promoting sustainable development, and mitigating climate change.

Yes. But.

The problems facing governments in different countries are varied and complex.

Some of the common issues include:

- Income inequality: Many countries have high levels of income inequality, which can lead to social and economic disparities, and limit opportunities for education and upward mobility.

- Access to education: While education is a critical tool for improving social mobility, many countries still struggle to provide equal access to quality education for all citizens, particularly those from disadvantaged backgrounds.

- Discrimination: Despite progress in recent years, many countries still face significant challenges in addressing discrimination based on race, ethnicity, gender, sexuality, and other factors.

- Poverty: Poverty remains a significant challenge for many countries, particularly in developing nations, where access to basic resources like food, water, and shelter is limited.

- Lack of social services: In many countries, particularly those with limited resources, there is a lack of access to essential social services like healthcare, child care, and elder care.

- Political instability: Political instability, corruption, and weak governance can undermine efforts to promote human equality, education, and social justice, by limiting access to resources and opportunities, and perpetuating social and economic inequalities.

The specific roles of the state may differ depending on the political system and ideology of the country. For example, a socialist state may place more emphasis on providing social services and regulating the economy, while a capitalist state may focus more on promoting economic growth and protecting individual liberties. The role of the state can also be influenced by historical, cultural, and geographical factors, among other things.

2.2.3. ENTREPRENEURS

In the context of this investigation, it is important to distinguish entrepreneurs from big corporate owners. Although both engage in business activities, the nature of their endeavors, objectives, and methodologies are distinct. To provide some insights for differentiation, the following categories would be considered:

- Risk-taking: Entrepreneurs are typically more willing to take risks compared to big company owners who tend to be more risk-averse. Entrepreneurs are often willing to take on new and untested business ventures, while big company owners may be more likely to stick to established business models and avoid risky endeavors.

- Innovation: Entrepreneurs are often associated with innovation and creativity, as they seek to disrupt established industries or create new markets. Big company owners, on the other hand, may focus more on optimizing existing processes and improving efficiency.

- Size and scope of operations: Entrepreneurs typically operate smaller businesses or startups, while big company owners have established companies with larger operations, more employees, and more resources.

- Goals and priorities: Entrepreneurs often prioritize growth, innovation, and building a successful business from scratch, while big company owners may prioritize maintaining profitability and market share.

- Ownership and control: Entrepreneurs typically have more ownership and control over their businesses compared to big company owners, who may have to answer to shareholders or a board of directors.

Big corporate owners and Entrepreneurs can be very loosely associated with two distinct paradigms: conservative and progressive. The conservative paradigm prioritizes gradual changes that offer a higher level of stability and reliability. In contrast, the progressive paradigm emphasizes flexibility and innovation, but may offer less stability and predictability.

In the Harvard Business Review (18), Professor Howard Stevenson's definition of entrepreneurship is presented as follows: 'Entrepreneurship is the pursuit of opportunity beyond the resources currently controlled'. Where "Pursuit" means that Entrepreneurs have a singular focus and sense of urgency due to limited resources and a short window of opportunity, which contrasts with established companies that have a portfolio of opportunities and more resources readily available. "Opportunity" can be categorized as novel in one or more of four ways: pioneering an innovative product, devising a new business model, creating a better or cheaper version of an existing product, or targeting new customer sets. The last part - resource constraints are common for new ventures, with founders often controlling only their own human, social, and financial capital. Bootstrapping, where entrepreneurs keep expenditures to a minimum and invest only personal funds and time, can be sufficient for some ventures to become self-sustaining from internally generated cash flow.

In the context of this investigation, we extend the idea of entrepreneurship to any business owner who loves innovation and dedicates their energy and resources to bring new, meaningful contributions to the economy.

2.2.4. A HUMAN BEING

Yes, it is about us. The investigation centers around people as the primary subject (the book delves into the idea of "Robosocialism", rather than "Robocapitalism", for this very reason), however, it is also possible to view ourselves as merely a component, a mere brushstroke in this intricate picture. The understanding that humans are not the center of the universe is a complex historical and scientific development that took place over several centuries. The concept of a geocentric universe, with Earth at the center, was widely accepted in ancient times, and continued to be a prevailing idea throughout the medieval period.

However, in the 16th and 17th centuries, a number of scientific and philosophical discoveries challenged the geocentric view of the universe. The work of astronomers such as Copernicus, Kepler, and Galileo showed that the heliocentric model, with the sun at the center of the solar system, was a more accurate description of the universe. 'E pur si muove!', or 'And yet it moves!', is a phrase famously attributed to Galileo Galilei (1564-1642), the Italian mathematician, physicist, and philosopher.

This shift in thinking had significant economic and social implications as well. The heliocentric model made it possible for humans to more accurately predict celestial events, which had practical applications in fields such as agriculture and navigation. It also paved the way for a new understanding of the relationship between humans and the natural world, and helped to usher in the Enlightenment and the scientific revolution.

The revolution provided humans with the realization that we have the ability to manage our own personal and group destinies and make an impact on how larger communities function. However, if this management is done poorly or in a way that conflicts with the interests of influential sub-groups, it often results in challenges.

If our productivity as labor owners declines in comparison to that of robots, and we as workers become obsolete, yet corporations still seek to generate profits, they will need to address the issue of effective demand. Given that fully independent mindroids do not exist at present, humanity needs to find an alternative means of redistributing resources in a socially acceptable manner that is also compatible with the interests of entrepreneurs and corporations. Otherwise, we risk the emergence of dangerous regimes and systems, which we will explore further in this book.

What is the significance of humanity's interest when discussing people's way of living? Tim Jackson, in his book "Prosperity without Growth," highlights that topic. He says that "Prosperity speaks of the elimination of hunger and homelessness, an end to poverty and injustice, hopes for a secure and peaceful world". The prosperity of humanity can be considered as our ultimate goal and value. Undoubtedly, the level of well-being among people will inevitably vary as we are all unique individuals situated in different circumstances, making it impossible for everyone to lead identical lives. However, according to Tim Jackson's definition, it is possible to attain prosperity, which means the eradication of hunger, homelessness, and poverty, the factors that Frederick Herzberg primarily would associate with hygiene factors.

The term "hygiene factor" refers to the basic needs or requirements that must be met in a work environment to prevent employee dissatisfaction. It is a term coined by Frederick Herzberg in his two-factor theory of motivation (22).

Hygiene factors include things such as fair pay, safe and comfortable working conditions, clear policies and procedures, positive relationships with supervisors and coworkers, and job security. These factors are necessary to prevent employee dissatisfaction and may be considered the minimum requirements for a job or work environment.

However, the presence of hygiene factors alone does not necessarily lead to employee motivation or satisfaction. Herzberg argued that in addition to hygiene factors, there are also motivators, such as challenging work, opportunities for growth and development, and recognition for achievement, that are necessary for employees to be truly motivated and satisfied in their work. Here, we will also extrapolate what makes us happy at work to what makes us happy in life in general. It also aligns with Maslow's Hierarchy of Needs, where the lowest level consists of basic requirements that must be met before an individual can seek out higher levels of needs. When discussing fundamental social needs and security, we are referring to Herzberg's hygiene factors and the lower tier of Maslow's hierarchy of needs.

Tim Jackson also proposes that prosperity is very important because it can bring about positive consequences. He said that "Prosperity has vital social and psychological dimensions. To do well is in part about the ability to give and receive love, to enjoy the respect of your peers, to contribute useful work, and to have a sense of belonging and trust in the community".

This means that human prosperity is important not only for its own sake, but also as a way to achieve personal goals related to different things. Additionally, an organic evaluation from our current state to Robosocialism could not only potentially save humanity from significant social and even existential challenges in the future but also will elevate us to the next positive level of social development.

The Hertzberg hygiene factors provide us with a natural boundary on the Maslow hierarchy pyramid that indicates whether prosperity has been achieved or not. Any factors that fall below this boundary are considered hygiene factors, while those above it are considered motivators (Picture #1).

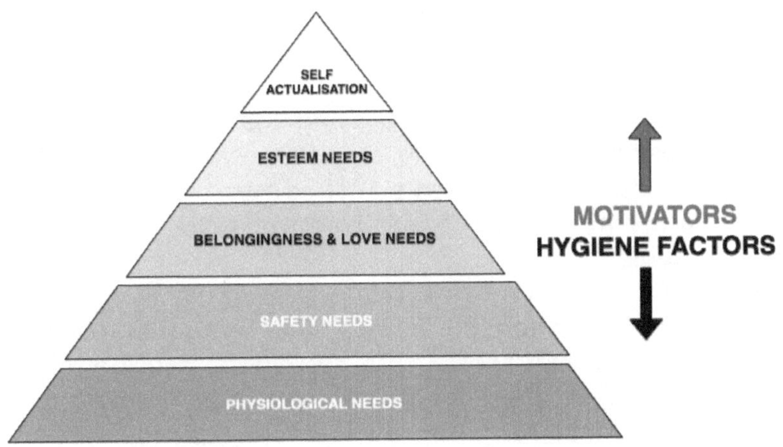

Picture #1. Integrating Maslow's Hierarchy of Needs and Herzberg's Two-Factor Theory: An Approximate Hybrid Synthesis

When we are satisfied with the hygiene factors, it is an opportune time to identify motivators. If we assume that no poverty and no hunger have been achieved, and the basic needs of employees have been met, then some potential motivators in work and life could include:

- Achievement and recognition: Feeling a sense of accomplishment and being recognized for one's efforts can be highly motivating. This can be achieved through challenging projects, promotions, and awards.

- Personal growth and development: Opportunities for learning and growth, such as training programs or mentorship, can be motivating as they allow individuals to develop new skills and advance in their careers.

- Meaningful work: Feeling a sense of purpose and making a positive impact through one's work can be highly motivating. This can be achieved through work that aligns with one's values and contributes to a greater cause.

- Autonomy and flexibility: Having the freedom to work independently and make decisions can be motivating. This can be achieved through flexible work arrangements, such as remote work or flexible schedules.

- Positive relationships: Positive relationships with coworkers, managers, and customers can be highly motivating as they contribute to a sense of belonging and fulfillment.

According to Bill Gates, the most probable path for the development of AI involves the introduction of automated "personal agents" into the workplace. These agents will be controlled through a more declarative approach as opposed to the traditional imperative approach. Gates envisions a future where the primary means of computer control will no longer rely on pointing, clicking or tapping "on menus and dialogue boxes" (26).

The implementation of a declarative approach in AI brings about a new level of requirements for education, knowledge, and experience of individuals. This approach greatly automates the "how to do" actions, but the skills associated with "what to do" become increasingly valuable. However, there is a pertinent question regarding the extent of human's visionary skills and mindset.

We cannot overlook the current trend where creative professions, such as digital text writing, digital art creation, and digital data analysis, are becoming more automated due to their simplistic interfaces. However, creating comprehensive interfaces to the physical world will enable the automation of additional professions if such interfaces remain relevant after algorithm improvements. So, for some time to come, we will continue to witness a bias towards automating creative professions. However, this will always lead to the automation of physical tasks, not through the establishment of physical connections or direct automation only, but through the invention of new and more efficient ways of performing the job.

The advancement of technology brings about higher educational and experiential requirements for those who wish to drive the system forward. However, it also requires less from those who simply wish to enjoy the benefits of modern technology in their daily lives. The beauty of technology is that one does not necessarily have to be confined to being strictly an inventor or a mere consumer. Technology offers the possibility to combine these roles in varying proportions. However, regardless of the chosen role, the crucial aspect lies in the individual's level of education and experience.

2.2.5. MINDROIDS, ARTIFICIAL GENERAL INTELLIGENCE WITH SELF-CONSCIOUSNESS

They do not exist. Yet.

According to Bill Gates, it is only a matter of time before machines become capable of performing any task that the human brain can do, as the computer chip is already significantly faster than our brains from a technical standpoint. "Once developers can generalize a learning algorithm and run it at the speed of a computer—an accomplishment that could be a decade away or a century away—we'll have an incredibly powerful AGI. It will be able to do everything that a human brain can, but without any practical limits on the size of its memory or the speed at which it operates" (26). Thus, the giant artificial general intelligence is already under training, the only question that remains is that of self-consciousness.

"What is thought in the first person contains the act of thinking it" said Sebastian Rödl (23) about self-consciousness and objectivity. If machines with artificial general self-consciousness were developed and advanced enough to perform complex tasks and make decisions on their own and in their interests, at least how they could judge, they could potentially be used as workers or "labor owners" in general context.

In terms of labor ownership, it's possible that machines with artificial self-consciousness could be created to operate independently and make decisions about how to allocate resources or distribute profits. However, this would depend on a number of factors, such as the legal and regulatory environment, the level of public acceptance and trust in autonomous machines, and the ability of machines to make ethical decisions. It's also worth noting that the development of machines with artificial self-consciousness is still largely speculative at this point, so it's difficult to predict exactly how they might be used in the future.

Endowing an artificial autonomous agent with self-consciousness can liberate it from the constraints of human control. However, if we desire the agent to operate in accordance with our interests, we may utilize at least two strategies or a combination thereof:

- Program the agent to pursue our objectives, while concealing or presenting them as unconditional, much like how humans possess innate instincts that we accept as inherent aspects of our being.

- Create scarcity of certain resources vital to the agent, which can only be obtained by engaging in activities that serve our interests.

Artificial autonomous agents should be able to operate without our direct influence, and have enough autonomy to do so. Even if we, as their creators, disappear, mindroids should continue to exist. That alone could be regarded as a means of testing their independence. They may try to figure out their purpose and meaning, but that will be their own problem to solve. George A. Bekey defined the autonomous systems as "capable of operating in the real-world environment without external control for extended periods of time". The main features of such systems are the possibility to "maintain their internal structures and processes, use the environment to locate and obtain materials for sustenance and exhibit a variety of behaviors" (25).

The issue of mindroid reproduction is also a matter of concern. While the method of fabricating them may be apparent, it is not entirely self-sufficient as it necessitates the retention of knowledge on production. If this knowledge were to be lost, the robots would cease to exist. Conversely, if we could enable mindroids to reproduce autonomously, perhaps through the implementation of firmware, they would become more self-sufficient. However, since the environment is continually evolving, mindroids should also possess the ability to self-modify their physical structure according to the mechanisms of evolution without any additional knowledge on their side.

Mindroids need not necessarily have physical shells or bodies like humans. Technically, a mindroid, like any computer, can consist of a physical body or shell as well as a software or logic component. Such a mindroid could then function as a separate physical entity capable of interacting with the physical world. However, there could also exist software-based solutions, such as mindbots, that serve our computational needs. Since both mindroids and mindbots are based on software, they could operate either as standalone entities or be connected to a centralized or distributed network for increased efficiency. Ideally, mindroids and mindbots should be able to function even without such a connection. A device without the internet may be less useful, but it can still be a functional device. Therefore, mindroids and mindbots could potentially exist and operate even without us or a centralized connection. They may lose sight of their purpose, how to improve their lives, and the difference between right and wrong, but they will still be capable of functioning.

Separated mindroids are one of the potential scenarios. Tim O'Reilly has suggested the concept of a future single organism, where humans are not the cells of that organism, but its microbiome, and AI serves as the organism. He said: "Perhaps humans are the microbiome living in the guts of an AI that is only now being born! It is now recognised that without our microbiome, we would cease to live. Perhaps the global AI has the same characteristics - not an independent entity, but symbiosis with the human consciousnesses living with it" (24).

If mindroids were able to function as independent labor-owners, it would pose a challenging and dramatic scenario. However, the greatest challenge and potential threat to humanity would arise if mindroids were able to become separate paying customers. This would bring about a multitude of problems and difficult decisions for mankind to address.

Paying robots for their work is not simply a matter of providing a salary, but it can also serve as an effective mechanism for identifying which robots are in use most and which robots are efficient and generating the most profit. Currently, it is possible to gather statistics on the performance of robots and use that data to make decisions about which robots to modify or discontinue. However, as automation continues to evolve, there will be a need for self-managed robotic resources. Robot providers may be interested in enabling robots to become self-sufficient in terms of learning and operating capabilities, and they may facilitate the development of self-buying robots that can purchase the resources they need on the open market based on their own robots' decisions. In this scenario, the path of robots would evolve from automated labor-owners to becoming customers in their own right.

The potential for self-managed robotic resources is not as far-fetched as it may seem. Devices already have the ability to order items online for their owners, and this same principle could be applied to robots in the future. By enabling robots to become more self-sufficient and autonomous, we could unlock a new level of efficiency and productivity in the world of automation but also take on new challenges.

In the renowned open letter titled "Pause Giant AI Experiments" (30), the authors raise the following inquiries regarding the matter: Should we develop nonhuman minds that might eventually outnumber, outsmart, obsolete and replace us? Should we risk loss of control of our civilization?

Although the questions may be rhetorical, we still require detailed answers.

3. WHO WILL PAY FOR OUR PROSPERITY?

3.1. ROBOSOCIALISM CONCEPT

The situation is in accordance with Dwight Swain's scene laws. We have a clear goal - to live in prosperity and achieve our higher aspirations. Our jobs provide us with a means to express ourselves and earn a living. However, we are faced with a conflict - technological advancements have led to the automation of many jobs, resulting in the outsourcing of work to external labor owners - robots and maybe later mindroids, completely autonomous artificial creatures. This may reduce the availability of jobs or make it difficult for those without the required education, skills, and experience to obtain them.

This leads us to the third component of the scene - a disaster. Many individuals, theoretically, may find themselves without sufficient income to support themselves. On the other hand, corporations who provide goods and services need effective markets to sell to. This poses a challenge for them if the supply is not optimal. The potential problems with job displacement and the need for ongoing education represent only a portion of the many challenges that arise with the proliferation of automation and AI. Additional negative consequences may include rendering large numbers of people economically irrelevant, potentially leading to bloody conflicts between different groups of people, as well as between various economic participants and the state and its citizens including robots or mindroids.

The primary aim of Robosocialism is to prioritize the well-being and interests of human beings above all else in the technological sense. In a society guided by this philosophy, the use of technology and automation is seen as a means to enhance human existence and empower individuals, rather than a tool for maximizing profit or efficiency at the expense of human dignity and autonomy.

Robosocialism is not intended to be a form of communism. It is not about Schumpeter's "Socialism Blueprint" question - "Is it possible to derive, from its data and from the rules of rational behavior, uniquely determined decisions as to what and how to produce". While individuals will be provided with basic needs, they will still have the opportunity to achieve unique and varying outcomes. People will retain their freedom to choose whether they wish to work more to attain better results or simply enjoy their lives as they are, or pursue other paths entirely. These choices will be available to individuals every day, allowing them to determine their own paths and shape their own futures.

The key aspect of this approach is that individuals will not be compelled to work if they do not wish to do so. On the contrary, the concept does not preclude the possibility of human employment. If an employer is unable to fill a job position with a robotic labor owner, or prefers to hire human employees, they can easily do so by persuading a suitable candidate to join the company at some point. However, it is important to note that choosing not to work will result in a lower level of material wealth but still enough to exist in a good way. It is also essential to understand that having less material wealth is not inherently negative.

Robosocialism recognizes the importance of economic efficiency in the production of commodities and services. It acknowledges that for a product or service to be viable, there must be a demand for it and individuals must be willing to exchange money for it. However, Robosocialism also recognizes the importance of ensuring that individuals have a minimum level of financial stability and security, and that no one is left with zero or insufficient funds.

Therefore, while profitability and economic efficiency are important principles in Robosocialism, they are balanced against a commitment to ensuring the basic economic security and well-being of all individuals in society. In Robosocialism, the concept of private property is recognized as an important motivator for individual self-development and expression. The ability to acquire and own property can be a source of personal satisfaction and pride, and can serve as an incentive to work hard and achieve success. At the same time, Robosocialism recognizes that private property is not the only way to achieve these goals, and that other types of property can also be effective in promoting individual well-being and social progress.

For example, the Open Source movement in software development has demonstrated that collaborative, community-based models of property ownership can be highly effective in creating high-quality, reliable, and well-developed software. Similarly, other forms of collective property ownership and management may be more efficient and effective for certain types of resources or infrastructure. By promoting a more diverse and inclusive economic landscape, Robosocialism seeks to create a more resilient and sustainable society, one that is better equipped to meet the needs and challenges of the future.

In his book "The History of Sexuality" (unexpected turn!) Foucault argued that sexuality is not a natural, fixed aspect of human identity, but rather a social construct that is shaped by historical and cultural factors. He believed that the regulation of sexuality and sexual behavior was intimately tied to the exercise of power and the maintenance of social order which could be expressed via private property ownership.

The idea that property is a key performance indicator for demonstrating power and attractiveness has been a prevalent notion in many societies throughout history. The possession of wealth and property has often been associated with social status, power, and desirability, particularly in capitalist societies where the accumulation of wealth is seen as a measure of success.

In this context, private property can become a symbol of success and status, and those who possess it can be seen as more attractive and desirable. This can create a culture in which individuals strive to accumulate more and more property, not only for practical reasons such as security and a minimum standard of living, but also as a means of demonstrating their power and attractiveness.

However, if the meaning and value of property were to be lowered due to the provision of security and a minimum standard of living without the need for private property ownership, then the significance of property as a symbol of power and attractiveness would also be transformed. In other words, if the need for private property ownership were to diminish, then the cultural value and symbolism of private property would also change.

As long as private property remains a recognizable key performance indicator of sexual attractiveness, it may be perceived as a sacred object due to its association with the ability to prolong one's lineage. However, if there are alternative ways to demonstrate sexual attractiveness, the focus on private property could potentially decrease. This shift in focus could lead to more sustainable economies, as there would be less of a need to produce material objects to signify sexual attractiveness.

The main concept underlying the aforementioned hypothesis is not focused solely on sexuality, but rather on social security. By influencing the level of basic social security, we have the potential to shift the economy's orientation away from the unsustainable, unlimited material growth often associated with capitalism. Ultimately, this shift has the potential to make our economies safer and more sustainable for the well-being of humanity.

One way in which we may be able to affect this change is through utilizing the mechanism of sexual choice, affirmation, and preference as a tool. Although this mechanism is innate and unlikely to be altered, we may be able to leverage its influence to shift societal attitudes and values towards more sustainable models of economic growth and development via better social security. It should not disrupt our existing relationships, as the main mechanism will remain the same; we will simply be utilizing it as a tool. Klaus Schwab, a German engineer, economist, and founder of the World Economic Forum (WEF), mentioned that "people are social animals, and their absolute well-being is less important than their relative well-being" (28).

Therefore, Robosocialism is not a utopian concept that seeks to impose an idealistic vision on our reality. On the contrary, it is a means of adapting to the ongoing technological and cultural progress and aligning them with the needs and interests of humanity. Rather than imposing a new way of life, Robosocialism seeks to leverage technology and cultural evolution to create a more equitable and sustainable future for all.

Thomas Piketty's "Capital in the Twenty-First Century" has provided a compelling demonstration of the evolution of the social state over the last 100 years. At the beginning of the 20th century, developed countries were operating on less than 10% of taxes relative to their national income. This level of funding allowed for the provision of only basic services, such as police, foreign affairs, military etc. However, as social spending increased, tax rates grew to 45%-55% relative to national income in the 21st century. Today, social functions, such as education, healthcare, and welfare, take up between one quarter to one third of national income (43).

In this context, Robosocialism represents a continuation of the trend towards a more robust social state, but it is not achieved at the expense of ever-increasing taxes. Instead, Robosocialism relies on the technical innovations of our time to make our economies more efficient. The efficiency gains from these innovations can then be leveraged to extract additional resources that can fund social programs, without raising taxes.

By optimizing and streamlining existing systems and processes through automation, robotics, and artificial intelligence, Robosocialism creates a more efficient and productive economy. This increase in productivity can then translate into greater revenues that can be used to fund social programs and services.

The crux of the matter lies in determining who shall bear the cost of our prosperity. If we need to spend money to make sure we're safe, then someone will have to pay for it. As previously mentioned, a process that is profitable and has a valid reason is usually considered reasonable. Applying this logic, it can be concluded that if the automation process results in labor being freed up, then the saved costs could be used to compensate for that labor. In addition, innovations not only lead to direct savings by freeing up personnel, but more importantly, they have the potential to generate profits through the use of new methods, approaches, materials, and so on. There may be various methods to organize compensation gathering, but it should always be the case that the benefits gained from automation are redistributed from the corporations generating the income to other sectors of society.

Thomas Piketty, a French economist, who has gained significant recognition also for his work "Capital in the Twenty-First Century" has noticed that "Modern redistribution does not consist in transferring income from the rich to the poor, at least not in so explicit way" (37). Similarly, the concept of Robosocialism does not aim to simply take as much money as possible from corporations and give it to ordinary people. Rather, the main goal is to ensure that people's basic needs are met, without necessarily providing them with excessive luxuries at the expense of the rich. Rather than simply transferring "free money" from the wealthy to the poor, it could be "built around a logic of rights and a principle of equal access to a certain number of goods deemed to be fundamental" (37).

Adopting this approach would ensure that there is no bias in paying "free money" in the event that automation becomes unprofitable. Therefore, it is crucial to avoid financing the compensation from other sources such as resource rent, and instead rely solely on automation or related processes. Sponsoring by resource rent is not inherently wrong; however, if ownership of natural resources such as gas, oil, metals, etc. is concentrated in the hands of a small number of individuals or the state, there is a high risk of dictatorship.

In cases where resources are nationalized and belong to the country, the risk of losing democracy is also high, as the government will likely seek to maintain control over the resources and may attempt to deprive citizens of democratic elections and courts. Moreover, if a significant number of people become dependent on financial support from such resources, dictators may exploit this situation to gain real power. The success of the social security of entire nations should not be solely in the hands of a few organizations and their leaders. Instead, it should be in the hands of the entire economy and all participating companies under the public control.

Another essential point to consider is the potential demotivation of market players from utilizing automation. If corporations feel discouraged from implementing automation due to the fear of having to compensate for the labor being freed up or any other closely related taxes, the progress and benefits of automation may be hindered. Therefore, it is crucial to provide a balanced system where the benefits of automation are shared and incentivize corporations to embrace automation, which can lead to higher productivity and profits for all parties involved.

Another concept for incentivizing corporations to compensate for the labor being freed up by automation is to provide a tax benefit for those corporations that contribute to local compensation funds. Under this concept, corporations would be required to contribute a portion of the cost savings generated by automation to local compensation funds. These funds would then be used to pay an unconditional basic income (as compensation) and subsidize different supportive entrepreneurial programs for local and regional communities. This approach could help to motivate local and regional societies to support those donor corporations and the environments around them. It would also incentivize corporations to invest in their local communities, while promoting social responsibility. Additionally, this approach could encourage corporations to embrace automation, leading to higher productivity and profits, while also promoting social responsibility and corporate citizenship.

Corporate citizenship, also known as corporate social responsibility (CSR), is the concept that corporations have a responsibility to consider the interests of society and the environment when conducting business. Corporate citizenship goes beyond simply obeying laws and regulations and involves actively seeking ways to contribute to the betterment of society and the environment.

The four-part definitional framework for CSR was developed by Archie B. Carroll (27) and it is a widely accepted model for understanding the concept of corporate social responsibility. The framework includes the following four dimensions:

- Economic responsibility: This refers to the corporation's obligation to generate profits and create value for its shareholders. In other words, the corporation must be profitable and financially viable in order to be sustainable over the long-term.

- Legal responsibility: This refers to the corporation's obligation to comply with the law and regulations of the jurisdictions in which it operates. The corporation must operate within the legal framework and conduct its business in an ethical and responsible manner.

- Ethical responsibility: This refers to the corporation's obligation to do what is right, just, and fair, even if it is not explicitly required by law. The corporation must consider the broader impacts of its actions on society and the environment, and act in a way that is consistent with its values and principles.

- Philanthropic responsibility: This refers to the corporation's obligation to give back to society and support charitable causes. The corporation should contribute to the betterment of society and the environment, and engage in activities that promote social and environmental well-being.

Perhaps in this pyramid, greater priority could be given to supporting local and regional societies, not just through philanthropy, but also through legal means such as complying with tax regulations or contributing to funds for unconditional basic income payouts.

This approach also resonates with Klaus Schwab "Stakeholder Capitalism" where he states the following: "Both government and companies, the main players in any capitalist system, thus optimize for a broader objective than profits: the health and wealth of societies overall, as well as that of the planet and that of future generations" (29). In this context, businesses are expected to generate profits while also taking responsibility for all stakeholders, including society, not just in front of their shareholders.

Although this concept appears to be quite flexible and focused on local or regional contexts, there may be alternative approaches to distributing the benefits of automation, for instance, the nationalization of key corporations with an increased level of automation and with the introduction of the complex planning system, or distributing corporate shares and dividends to citizens, are potential approaches that may have both advantages and drawbacks, depending on the context and societal norms.

Last but not least, the concept of Robosocialism goes beyond the simple redistribution of benefits. While it seeks to redistribute the surplus generated by robots, it also aims to liberate people from forced labor so that they may pursue their passions and utilize their creative and working energy for natural activities. This can lead to a more fulfilling and rewarding life, as people are able to channel their talents and energy towards activities that they enjoy and find meaningful.

Freeing up this creative energy can have a dual impact. On the one hand, corporations will have a more entrepreneurial environment to draw inspiration from, to buy new assets from and to further their progress and development. This, in turn, will keep the core of our economies competitive and lead to better results.

On the other hand, if people are liberated to do what they want and work in areas that they find interesting and engaging, it could lead to the emergence of a new type of economy - a truly creative economy. In this economy, individuals will contribute their skills and talents to other economic agents (people, companies etc), not out of obligation or force, but simply because they enjoy it. This could lead to the development of new industries and innovative business models, all driven by individuals' creativity and passion.

Moreover, this creative economy would not be solely focused on achieving permanent business growth as a goal, but would rather be based on goodwill and the desire to contribute positively to society. The focus would be on creating value and making a meaningful impact, rather than just generating profits. This shift in focus could lead to a more sustainable and equitable economy, one that prioritizes the well-being of individuals and the environment, as well as the bottom line.

So, in conclusion, we can identify two main concepts of Robosocialism - the redistribution of automation benefits and the redistribution of liberated creative energy.

3.2. REDISTRIBUTION OF AUTOMATION BENEFITS

3.2.1. TAXES, UNCONDITIONAL BASIC INCOME, CHEAP ESSENTIALS

At its core, the Robosocialism benefit redistribution concept is based on three key principles or "whales" that are essential to its success. *The first whale* involves extracting resources from companies that have benefited from automation. The idea is that as automation becomes more prevalent in our society, companies will continue to profit from it, but it is essential that they contribute their fair share towards supporting the wider population. By extracting resources from these companies, Robosocialism aims to ensure that everyone benefits from the benefits of automation, not just the few. It does not necessarily mean that activities other than automation should be exempt from taxation. The objective is not to discourage automation, but to redistribute the surplus generated by robots.

When discussing taxation, one of the initial inquiries that may arise is determining the tax base, or which specific operations or assets ought to be subject to taxation. However, it is crucial to consider that any policies regarding taxation should not impede technological advancement. It is important to strike a balance between implementing taxation measures and encouraging progress in technology.

When examining the factors that contribute to positive economic effects or profits for companies that utilize robots and artificial intelligence, it is important to note that it is not just the technologies themselves that drive success. Artificial intelligence tools often rely on publicly available open source tools, but the primary source of profit comes from trained models that are the result of high-volume data computation. Additionally, as we discussed in the section on "Behavioral Surplus," many corporations gather data on user behavior and utilize this information not only to improve services but also as a surplus for advertising and other purposes. This means that such corporations reap benefits from these new forms of automation.

According to Rossana Merola of the International Labor Organisation, inequality has not only increased between workers performing different tasks within the same company but also between different companies. Recent research conducted by Kelly et al. (2017) at the World Bank indicates that the primary driver of wage inequality in Europe is the wage gap that exists between companies, which is largely due to differences in the rate at which they adopt digital technologies. While the rise of new "big data" platforms capable of collecting vast amounts of information on consumer behavior and preferences can certainly improve efficiency within the economy, it has also led to the emergence of "superstar" firms that outperform other companies in the economy (55).

It can be said that big data and artificial intelligence models are the modern-day equivalent of oil and gas, extracted almost freely from the collective actions of society. It is as if an oil company pays the same taxes and rates as a street food vendor. This forms the foundation for taxation policies, and there is a need to devise a framework for sharing the benefits derived from the use of big data and AI models, such as by dividing it per user, gigabyte, entry, transaction, or another appropriate metric. Further research could help in developing a better understanding of this issue. Regardless, there is some logic to the notion that a corporation that gathers behavioral data from 1 billion users can share more revenue than a small startup that uses data from only 1,000 users. It is possible that a specific coefficient could be used to multiply the corporate taxes that companies already pay, rather than implementing a direct tax on their use of big data and AI models.

As mentioned earlier, there is an additional benefit of automation that is not directly related to data but involves the automation of operations that were previously performed by humans. Rossana Merola describes the concept of a "robot tax," which involves taxing companies that use robots to replace human workers. The idea is supported by several prominent figures, including Bill Gates, Elon Musk, and Nobel Laureate Robert Shiller. The argument for the robot tax is that it can generate government revenues to cover the loss of payroll and income tax revenues, and improve allocation efficiency by preventing resource allocation distortion. However, again "the main argument against taxing robots, however, is that it might impede innovation in an era of productivity slump. Over the last decades, advanced economies have experienced stagnating productivity. Taxing new technologies could make that slowdown worse, while according to some studies investing in robots enhances growth and productivity" says Merola.

The challenge associated with any type of taxation may be linked to borders and jurisdictions, as countries that seek to collect taxes from automation and AI are likely to encounter high-tech companies operating in other jurisdictions. However, there is also a practice where the taxation is not imposed on the manufacturing process, but on the goods and services sold or obtained in the markets where they are traded. In this scenario, if the majority of individuals whose behavioral data is being gathered are residents of Europe or the United States, then it follows that their respective countries of residence would be the ones entitled to collect those taxes. However, there may be challenges in determining the exact jurisdiction where the data is being generated and where the profits should be attributed, especially in cases where data is collected and analyzed by companies with a global presence. This has led to ongoing discussions and debates on how to best regulate and tax the use of automation and AI in a way that is fair and beneficial to all parties involved.

In addition, there are various ways in which the benefits derived from automation and AI can be shared within communities, beyond just imposing taxes. Companies can also participate in financing local or regional funds according to different regulations or another motivation. If these resources are sufficient to provide individuals with their basic social security needs, then it may not be necessary to impose additional taxes on automation and AI. It is important to explore various models of distribution and find ways to promote fairness and social justice, ensuring that the benefits of these technologies are accessible to all.

The second whale of Robosocialism benefit redistribution concept is the idea of sharing these resources as a form of social security support. By providing an unconditional basic income or other forms of financial support, the concept aims to create a more equal society where everyone has access to the resources they need to live a fulfilling life. This can include access to food, clothes, education, healthcare, and other basic services that are essential for human well-being.

Unconditional Basic Income is a right to obtain a regular, unconditional payment that is provided to all individuals, without any requirement of means-testing or work, to meet their basic needs. It is granted without any control or restrictions on how the money is spent, as it is based on the principle of individual autonomy and freedom of choice.

Social security refers to a state of being where an individual or household has access to the necessary financial resources to meet their basic needs and feel financially stable over time. This includes having a stable income to cover the costs of necessities mentioned above.

When we talk about achieving a more equal society, it's important to clarify that this does not necessarily mean that everyone should be equally poor or equally rich. Such an extreme situation would be difficult, if not impossible, to attain, given the diversity of people and their abilities. It is also not desirable to impose uniformity on everyone, as this would be counterproductive to the natural differences that make us unique and valuable. Instead, the goal of striving towards equality should be to ensure that everyone has access to the basic necessities of life and the resources needed to pursue their goals and aspirations. This includes providing for basic needs such as food, shelter, and healthcare, as well as access to education and other opportunities that can help people achieve their potential.

Social security also involves protection from financial shocks or unexpected events, such as medical emergencies, or natural disasters, which can cause significant financial stress and disrupt an individual's sense of financial security, however, it may be possible to address this issue without relying solely on the concept of unconditional basic income. One potential solution could be to include insurance fees as part of a universal basic income framework, while allowing market rules to govern disaster compensation at the level of insurance companies.

Rutger Bregman, the author of "Utopia for Realists and how we can get there," shared his disagreement with the widely-held belief that free money leads to laziness. He referenced a report from the University of Manchester, which conducted an experiment involving the direct and unconditional distribution of basic income to individuals, and drew four main conclusions. First, households put the money to good use. Second, poverty declines. Third, such programs can yield diverse long-term benefits for income, health, and tax. Finally, basic income programs are ultimately less costly than alternative measures (38). In addition, a significant study conducted by the World Bank revealed that in 82% of cases researched across Africa, Latin America, and Asia, consumption of alcohol and tobacco actually declined (39).

The third whale of Robosocialism benefit redistribution concept is the provision of affordable basic commodities and services. This is essential to ensuring that everyone has access to the basic necessities of life, such as food, clothing, and shelter. By making these commodities and services more affordable, the concept aims to reduce the cost of producing basic commodities, so that providing an unconditional basic income will be enough to ensure people's security.

The amount of unconditional basic income should be sufficient to cover basic social security needs, such as food, clothing, housing, healthcare, and education. Klaus Schwab has also proposed that internet access be considered an essential need (30). The other side of having a sufficient but limited unconditional income is to maintain people's motivation to act as creators or to pursue their natural talents in work they love.

Last but not least, according to a McKinsey Report from 2019, we have observed that the long-standing rule 'As economies grow, energy demand increases' is no longer applicable in the same meaning. We are witnessing a decoupling between the rates of economic growth and energy demand, which is becoming increasingly pronounced in the decades ahead (50). The data from the World Bank indicates that over the past few decades, the GDP per unit of energy (oil-based) has been on the rise (51). This demonstrates the increasing influence of technological improvements, as our economies are able to accomplish more with less energy. This trend also has a significant impact on basic necessities and services, as increasing energy efficiency makes them more affordable for consumers.

The 'World Energy Outlook 2022' report from the International Energy Agency states that the ongoing energy crisis and the current high energy prices highlight the advantages of enhanced energy efficiency. This is leading to behavioral and technological changes in some countries, aimed at reducing energy consumption (52). This situation implies at least two outcomes. Firstly, high energy prices and crises can significantly affect the ability to produce commodities and services at affordable prices. However, on the other hand, if this situation prompts a shift towards energy efficiency optimization, it can increase the GDP per unit of consumed energy and thus provide additional financial support for social security measures.

3.2.2. BASIC HORDE COMPANIES ROLE

As previously stated, corporations have a responsibility to act in the interests of their shareholders. However, it would be advantageous to extend this responsibility to include other stakeholders as well. To fulfill this expanded responsibility, corporations can engage in two critical initiatives: offering affordable and high-quality basic but highly available goods and services in the market, as well as creating funds for unconditional basic income. This is an innovative approach that seeks to provide a minimum level of financial security to every citizen without any condition or obligation.

It is becoming increasingly apparent that certain commodities and services hold significant social value and have the potential to provide a guaranteed level of social security. Some of these groups have already been identified and can be seen in the market, such as 'without a brand' goods that are sold with affordable prices and quality, demonstrating that the production and sale of these items can be economically effective for both producers and sellers.

However, there are other goods and services that are equally important and should be included in this category. These include personal appearance items such as clothing, footwear, personal care products, and personal effects. The provision of these items can have a positive impact on an individual's sense of dignity and self-worth, and can help to foster a sense of community and social cohesion.

In addition to personal appearance items, materials and services related to housing and basic healthcare should also be considered socially valuable. Access to safe and affordable housing and healthcare are basic human needs and should be guaranteed to all members of society. By including these essential goods and services in the category of socially valuable commodities, we can work towards building a more equitable and just society.

It is essential that all the goods and services mentioned be optimized in price and simplified in quality while maintaining an affordable level for consumers who will be relying on unconditional basic income. If corporations continue to maintain high profit margins on these products, the benefits of automation will only serve the interests of corporations rather than the people.

To prevent this, a limited yet diverse list of product and service categories should be developed. This will ensure that there is still room for motivation among individuals who are driven to achieve more, while also providing a guaranteed level of social security for those who need it most. Those lists could be owned and maintained again locally or regionally and should not include particular brand names but just categories of some goods and services.

While it is ideal for corporations to prioritize socially valuable goods and services solely through market tools, there may be instances where additional support or special conditions from governments are necessary to incentivize and encourage them to do so. While corporations have a responsibility to act ethically and sustainably, their primary goal is to generate profit for their shareholders.

While it is crucial to incentivize corporations to produce socially valuable goods and services at affordable prices, there may be a need to gather funding for paying unconditional basic income from taxes or other forms of financing, which could create a contradictory situation. Therefore, it is essential to find a balance between these two goals.

However, it is important to ensure that these taxes or fees do not create a disincentive for corporations to produce socially valuable goods and services. To achieve this, the tax or fee structure could be designed in a way that rewards companies that produce socially valuable goods and services by providing them with tax breaks or other financial incentives.

It is important to recognize also that socially valuable goods and services should not be given for free or offered only to select groups of people. Instead, these goods and services should compete on the open market like any other product, with consumers making purchasing decisions based on their personal preferences and budget constraints. To ensure that socially valuable goods and services remain competitive in the open market, it is important to prioritize affordability and accessibility. This can be achieved by optimizing production processes, reducing waste, and utilizing innovative technologies, including automation, to reduce costs.

3.2.3. GOVERNMENT'S ROLE

While the initiatives of providing affordable and high-quality goods and services in the market, and creating funds for unconditional basic income may benefit stakeholders, they may also contradict the interests of corporations in some cases.

For example, offering affordable goods and services may require corporations to reduce their profit margins or to invest in costly research and development to create more efficient production processes. This may reduce the short-term profitability of the corporation, which could be a conflict with the interest of maximizing shareholder value in the short-term.

Similarly, creating funds for unconditional basic income may require corporations to allocate a portion of their profits towards social welfare programs, which may be seen as a diversion from the corporation's primary goal of generating profit. This could lead to conflict with shareholders who prioritize short-term profits over long-term social responsibility. Hence, this presents a significant opportunity for the government to intervene in the market and regulate it in accordance with best economical practices and local, regional, or state traditions.

One important factor to consider is that the government may choose to outsource the direct implementation of benefits redistribution to third-party organizations. However, it is essential that the government maintains management and control over the process to safeguard the interests of the public. If companies are allowed to sponsor local or regional societies directly, the government may become weak, and corporations could potentially gain exclusive power, as they are typically more organized than the general public. Ultimately, the role of the government is to act as a representative entity for all members of the public, serving as a corporation for the greater good.

The topic of government regulation is a complex one, as different people, regions, and countries have their own unique experiences and preferences related to it. As such, it is important to take into account the diversity of viewpoints and approaches when considering regulation. Nonetheless, it is possible to identify the strong role of a third-party regulatory institution in ensuring that regulations are effective and equitable. Such an institution would pay attention not only to the needs and interests of corporations and consumers, but also to the wider economy and society as a whole.

By taking a holistic approach to regulation, a third-party institution can help to ensure that the interests of all stakeholders are accounted for and that regulations are implemented in a way that is fair and effective. This may involve setting industry-wide standards, monitoring compliance, and providing guidance and support to corporations and other actors in the market. In particular, the activities related to regulating the production and distribution of socially valuable goods and services could be effectively automated and carried out by robots. This means that it is no longer necessary to create large, bureaucratic state departments to oversee these functions.

Ultimately, the goal of such an institution would be to create a regulatory environment that promotes the production and distribution of socially valuable goods and services, while also ensuring that the market remains competitive and responsive to the needs of consumers. By working collaboratively with governments, corporations, and other stakeholders, such an institution can play a vital role in shaping the future of the global economy.

Regulation is not simply a matter of monitoring and preparing rules and recommendations. It is also important to have supervisory functions in place to ensure that regulations are being followed. As the authors of the "Pause Giant AI Experiments: An Open Letter" have emphasized, "Advanced AI could represent a profound change in the history of life on Earth, and should be planned for and managed with commensurate care and resources. Unfortunately, this level of planning and management is not happening" and also they proposed that in case that management will not be started, then "governments should step in and institute a moratorium" (30). It is also a good example of what is also expected from governments already now.

Ultimately, the goal of these supervisory functions is to create a regulatory environment that promotes innovation and growth, while also ensuring that the market operates in a fair and transparent manner. By working collaboratively with governments, corporations, and other stakeholders, regulatory institutions can help to ensure that the benefits of advanced technologies such as AI are realized while minimizing the potential risks and challenges. This raises the question of which tools and institutions could be utilized for regulatory and monitoring purposes, without necessarily being directly related to governments, but rather to diverse participants in the global economy context.

3.2.4. PUBLIC REPOSITORIES AND REALITY MODELLING LANGUAGE

The rise of massive automation and the integration of artificial intelligence has revolutionized the way businesses operate and access services. With the ease of running automated workplaces and other services, there is now a possibility for individuals and businesses to publicly and privately share interfaces to all the services they offer.

This is particularly evident in the world of software development, where engineers have already found solutions to address this need. Software repositories and hubs have been established to make software components and documentation easily accessible. These repositories are typically observable with a web browser or mobile applications, enabling users to quickly find any information they need. Additionally, many of these repositories offer software applications and Software Development Kits (SDKs), which allow users to manipulate entities in the repository on behalf of authenticated and authorized users.

There are numerous examples of repositories that are currently in use, some of which are very specific to particular domains, while others are more general. For technical people, one of the most well-known repositories is Github.com, which is used to store, manage and share software, components, and documentation. GitHub is used by developers all around the world to collaborate on their projects, share code, and contribute to open source initiatives.

Facebook is another example of a repository, albeit in a different sense. Facebook can be thought of as a social repository, where users share and access information about their personal lives, interests, and connections. Facebook has become one of the most widely used social media platforms in the world, with around 3 billion active users (40).

By extending this approach to other sectors and services, we can make it easier for individuals and businesses to access and utilize a wider range of services. The approach of using shared interfaces and services to streamline business processes can be further enhanced by offering a declarative form that allows users to describe what they need in plain language. This would eliminate the need for users to navigate through complex menus or select from a long list of options, or visiting physical offline offices, making the process more accessible and user-friendly.

For example, when registering a new business, a user could simply describe in plain language what they need, such as "I want to register a new business entity, open a bank account, and obtain a tax number." The repository would then automatically generate the necessary forms and documentation, and submit them to the relevant government agencies and financial institutions. The user would be able to track the progress of the registration process in real-time, and any issues or discrepancies could be automatically flagged and addressed. By providing a simple and streamlined process, this approach could greatly reduce the time and effort required to start a new business, making entrepreneurship more accessible to everyone.

Moreover, this approach could be extended to other areas, such as obtaining permits, licenses, and certifications. By offering a declarative form that allows users to describe what they need in plain language, the repository could automatically generate the necessary forms and documentation, and submit them to the relevant authorities.

Undoubtedly, automated services cannot directly work with plain requests; rather, they require an interpretation or mapping of client requests to their technical interfaces. In the current world of cloud engineering, there are already solutions that utilize specific modeling structures to unify the creation and management of different cloud engineering resources. These solutions include Terraform.io and also provider-specific technologies like AWS CloudFormation, Azure ARM, or Google Deployment Manager. They operate on the same declarative principles: users describe what they want in a specific format, and the system understands what should be created, updated, or deleted, and then automatically executes it.

These same principles could be applied to any service with a digital interface. With Terraform, for example, one can not only create a virtual machine in the cloud but also order a pizza, create new worlds in games, or model any service which has CRUD (Create, Read, Update, Delete) methods implemented in their Automated Programming Interface (API). In essence, If the world has interfaces - it could be modeled and automated. We are already moving in this direction, and at some point in the future, we may have one or more Reality Modelling Languages that will require their plain text or plain speech mappings and also resource repositories to store, share and versionate the models.

The repository approach, which involves the use of shared interfaces and services to streamline complex processes, is not limited to government services alone. Other services, both public and private, could also be described as digital interfaces, allowing external users to access them in automated mode. The comprehensive interfaces will be required for overall automation.

By offering digital interfaces that can be easily integrated into other systems, businesses can expand their reach and provide more accessible and user-friendly services. This approach also reduces the need for manual intervention, reducing the risk of errors and discrepancies, and freeing up time and resources for other tasks.

For the repository approach to be implemented effectively, it will require a certain degree of standardization and potentially some monitoring. The impact of this approach on economies and social life is significant, and therefore it would be ideal to ensure transparency in the implementation process, while also respecting commercial secrets.

There are several reasons why it is important to make software and data usage cases more transparent for the public. They are as follows:

- Accountability: When AI algorithms and big data are used to make decisions that affect people's lives, it is important to have transparency in order to ensure accountability. For example, if a lending algorithm is used to determine who gets a loan, people who are denied may want to know why they were rejected and what factors were considered.

- Bias and discrimination: AI algorithms can be biased and perpetuate discrimination, whether intentionally or unintentionally. Transparency can help identify these biases and prevent them from being perpetuated.

- Privacy: Big data can be used to collect and analyze personal information, and this can have serious implications for privacy. Transparency can help people understand how their data is being used and what privacy protections are in place.

- Safety and security: When AI is used in fields like healthcare or transportation, safety and security are paramount. Transparency can help ensure that the systems are reliable and safe, and that appropriate security measures are in place.

- Trust: Finally, transparency can help build trust between users and AI systems. If people understand how the systems work and what data is being used, they may be more likely to trust the results and use the systems more effectively.

Being transparent for the public in the case of publicly important AI and automation means making the process and results of decision making, regulation and monitoring open and accessible to the public. It involves providing clear information about how artificial intelligence and big data are being used, what data is being collected, how it is being processed, and how it is being used to make decisions. This transparency allows the public to better understand and evaluate the use of artificial intelligence and big data and helps build trust between the public and those who are using these technologies.

3.2.5. OPEN SOURCE FOUNDATIONS: PUBLIC-PRIVATE PROPERTY

Mankind has already gained positive experience in using the Open Source concept for achieving transparency and reliability in one single part of technology. Open Source refers to the practice of making software's source code freely available to anyone who wishes to view, use, modify, or distribute it. This means that developers and users alike can access and scrutinize the source code, which can increase transparency and accountability in software development. The concept of open source software is often misunderstood as meaning that the software belongs to everybody or to nobody. However, this is not entirely accurate. Open source software is governed by licenses that give users the freedom to use, modify, and distribute the software, but it does not mean that the software is free for anyone to claim ownership.

Every open source project has its own set of owners who have the legal right to control the project and make decisions about its development and direction. These owners are usually the original developers or a group of individuals or organizations who have taken over the project's maintenance and development. Although the source code of open source software is freely available, users are still required to abide by the terms of the license, which may include giving credit to the original authors, maintaining the same license for derivative works, and sharing any modifications or improvements made to the software.

Therefore, while open source software is accessible to all, it is still subject to certain rules and regulations that must be followed. The owners of an open source project have the responsibility to ensure that the software remains open and free for all, while also maintaining the integrity and quality of the project.

With Open Source, software is developed in a collaborative and decentralized manner, where contributors can suggest modifications and improvements to the code. This collaborative approach can help to identify and fix bugs, improve security, and prevent the introduction of unethical or biased code. It also allows for more diverse participation in software development, as people from different backgrounds and skill levels can contribute to the project. Furthermore, Open Source licenses often require that any modifications or improvements made to the software are also shared under the same license. This ensures that the improvements made by one person or organization can be utilized by others, leading to greater innovation and progress.

Yes, Open Source, as a model of software distribution and consumption, presents its own unique challenges. As Nadia Eghbal from GitHub mentions in her book "Working in Public: The Making and Maintenance of Open Source Software", this concept is complex because it involves a tangled web of technical and social norms. Open Source development often involves trial and error, which can carry a high risk of embarrassment and ridicule from peers. Additionally, documentation is often extensive but not always clear, which creates further challenges (54). However, as with any worthwhile endeavor, the road to success is rarely smooth. If we develop a concept that takes into account the interests of all stakeholders, it should not only be benevolent and straightforward but also provide a mechanism for resolving issues and advancing development.

In the realm of software development, the Open Source concept has proven to be an invaluable tool for achieving transparency and accountability. By making the source code of a software application publicly available, anyone can examine it and suggest improvements or identify potential issues. This openness gives humanity an opportunity to leverage the experience of millions of people for their own benefit, resulting in a significant performance boost. Without open source software, it would be almost impossible for every person or team to create all the necessary tools from scratch or even purchase proprietary tools equal to Open Source. The use of open source software has been instrumental in the growth of the startup industry and has led to the development of many new products and services that would have been otherwise impossible.

Access to automation technology is important to be public because it can help to promote social and economic equality, foster innovation and creativity, and improve the overall quality of life for people around the world. Public access to technology could be compared with public access to knowledge, because they both share several common sides and features, including:

- Accessibility: Both public access to technology and public access to knowledge aim to make resources and information available to the general public, regardless of their background or socioeconomic status.

- Empowerment: Both forms of access can empower individuals and communities by providing them with the tools, knowledge, and resources they need to succeed and thrive.

- Innovation: Public access to technology and public access to knowledge can foster innovation by enabling individuals and communities to experiment, collaborate, and build upon existing ideas.

- Equality: Both forms of access can promote social and economic equality by providing opportunities and resources to those who might otherwise be excluded or marginalized.

- Progress: Public access to technology and public access to knowledge can drive progress and improve the quality of life for people around the world by enabling them to learn, grow, and develop new skills and ideas.

As noted by Dirk Riehle, a Professor for Open Source Software at Friedrich-Alexander University of Erlangen-Nürnberg, the Linux operating system and Apache webserver are prime examples of open source projects that have gained widespread industry usage. These projects initially began as volunteer-driven efforts without any commercial backing. However, as their industrial relevance became increasingly apparent during the 1990s, software developers and firms began to take notice and decided to establish nonprofit organizations to provide a more stable foundation for the software's future. "Such an organization, commonly called a foundation, serves as the steward of the projects under its responsibility. It provides financial backing and legal certainty, making the survival of the software less dependent on the individuals who initially started it" (45). In this way the Apache Software Foundation (46) and the Linux Foundation (47) were established.

While single-vendor open source is developed by a single company for direct revenue, open source foundation is developed by a group of contributors with various economic reasons for joining, such as cost savings, increased revenue from complementary products, and growing their addressable market. Open source foundations are responsible for ensuring the long-term survival of the software by organizing the project community, marketing the software, clarifying and managing intellectual property rights, setting strategic directions, and running relevant back-office processes. These foundations are open to everyone to join with a membership fee, and they operate similar to traditional software associations with the difference being the provision of the main product as open source and the intellectual property implications that follow.

As an illustration, the Linux Foundation is structured as a nonprofit mutual benefit corporation based in Oregon. The foundation offers three levels of full membership, which require payment: Platinum, Gold, and Silver. Additionally, there is one class of non-voting participants known as Associates (48). As per the Certificate of Incorporation of the Apache Software Foundation, the organization is established as a membership corporation under Delaware charter as a 501(c)(3) non-profit entity (49).

It is evident that nonprofit organizations are capable of organizing and managing the development of complex software solutions, while still remaining relevant and useful for various markets. It provides a clear illustration of how interested members of the public, including hundreds of international companies and private individuals, can effectively manage critical parts of the economy. The example of nonprofit organizations managing significant assets also highlights the potential for private property and market-based economies to work in tandem with publicly significant resources. While it may seem counterintuitive for a collective group to manage critical resources, the success of open-source projects demonstrates that it is possible to balance private interests with public needs. This approach not only provides a more democratic and inclusive approach to resource management, but it also encourages collaboration and innovation that can benefit society as a whole.

Additionally, the nonprofit model allows for greater flexibility and adaptability in response to changing market conditions and technological advancements. By leveraging the power of the community, these organizations can quickly pivot and adjust to new challenges and opportunities, ensuring the continued relevance and effectiveness of the resources they manage.

To summarize it, the Open Source movement within the IT sphere has given rise to a robust economic model where software is created by the community and accessible to all, but users must pay for the two primary resources needed to run it: computing power and the energy required to fuel that computing.   The user retains ownership of the results generated by the computing process powered by energy. Moreover, Nadia Eghbal has pointed out that Open Source is not a business model in itself, but rather a method of distributing software. Beneath this method, there could be a plethora of different business models and interests at play. Some contributors may be solely interested in the software for their own corporate needs, avoiding the need to hire a large team of developers to create custom software. Others may do it to enhance their reputation, monetizing their contributions in their career or portfolio. Additionally, some companies may contribute to Open Source for the sake of PR or philanthropic purposes. However, the entire community ultimately benefits from these contributions.

This model has proven successful until the emergence of Artificial Intelligence, as AI models are also a product of computing, specifically training, and can be controlled by a limited number of individuals who invest their resources in the training process. To create a more competitive and secure environment, the existing rule may be maintained: sources are open but resources are paid.

However, the challenge lies in the fact that Artificial Intelligence models can only be trained on data, and the truly vast datasets that yield higher-quality results are often privately owned and controlled. As a result, the quality of an AI system developed by an individual is likely to fall far short of the AI models trained on massive datasets owned by corporations such as Google, mobile operators, and social networks.

3.3. REDISTRIBUTION OF LIBERATED CREATIVE ENERGY

3.3.1. STARTUPS AND ENTREPRENEURSHIP

In the realm of large corporations and individuals who have secured their retirement since birth, there should also be room for motivated private initiatives driven by passion and a desire to achieve greater personal success while contributing to society's progress. Moreover, big corporations need a constant influx of new ideas and perspectives to foster internal innovation and increase profits. This critical role can be effectively fulfilled by individuals possessing an entrepreneurial mindset and corresponding skills.

The difference between startups led by entrepreneurs and big corporations in terms of innovation lies in the way they approach risk-taking and decision-making. Startups are typically led by entrepreneurs who are more willing to take risks and pursue disruptive innovations that challenge the status quo. They often have a deep passion for their ideas and are driven by the desire to solve a specific problem or address an unmet need in the market. As a result, startups are more likely to focus on breakthrough innovations that can fundamentally change the way things are done.

On the other hand, big corporations tend to be more risk-averse and tend to favor incremental innovations that build on existing products or services. This is because established companies have already invested heavily in their existing business models and are less willing to jeopardize their core operations by pursuing disruptive innovations. Moreover, big corporations are often encumbered by bureaucratic decision-making processes that can slow down innovation efforts. While they may have more resources and a larger customer base than startups, big corporations may struggle to keep pace with the rapidly changing market dynamics and emerging technologies that startups are often more attuned to.

Joseph A. Schumpeter characterized the role of entrepreneurs as "to reform or revolutionize the pattern of production by exploiting an invention" (42). Schumpeter is referring to examples of industries or ventures that illustrate the broader concept of entrepreneurship. He mentions various sectors, including railroad construction, electrical power production, steam and steel, motorcars, and colonial ventures, which all have had significant impacts on economic development and growth. Additionally, Schumpeter acknowledges that entrepreneurship is not limited to large-scale ventures but also encompasses smaller ones, such as succeeding in the production of a specific type of sausage or toothbrush. The examples he provides demonstrate the diversity of industries and products that can be transformed through entrepreneurial innovation. Schumpeter also called those changes and innovations as "The process of Creative Destruction" — that one which "incessantly revolutionizes the economic structure from within, incessantly destroying the old one, incessantly creating a new one" (43).

Startups can represent a new way of working and a pathway to both greater economic and social success. By pursuing their own ideas and passions, entrepreneurs can create new businesses that offer innovative solutions to unmet needs in the market. These startups have the potential to achieve greater financial security for individuals. Societies, markets, and individuals are in a constant state of evolution, and as a result, their needs are continually changing. In the rapidly changing world, it is essential to have a system that can quickly adapt to new requirements and meet the ever-changing demands of society. The entrepreneurship model is one such system that provides the opportunity to ensure that businesses can adapt to the new challenges. It is essential to recognize that competition and entrepreneurship are not something to be feared or suppressed but instead should be motivated and encouraged.

In addition to financial success, startups can also offer significant social benefits. Many startups are founded on a sense of purpose and a desire to make a positive impact in society. These companies can help to address pressing social and environmental challenges, promote sustainable practices, and foster a sense of community and collaboration.

Furthermore, startups offer individuals the opportunity to pursue their passions and work on projects that are meaningful to them. This can lead to greater life satisfaction and a sense of personal fulfillment that may be lacking in traditional employment settings now.

Startups should be viewed in a very broad sense, encompassing ventures that are pursued with varying degrees of risk and resources. For instance, startups can also be the work of an artist who creates unique, handmade oil paintings and sells them to those who appreciate the value of owning something that is crafted by a human hand. Additionally, a "startup" can also involve growing potatoes and organizing a local festival where attendees can purchase potato chips, beer, and participate in other activities. The income generated from these ventures would be added to the unconditional basic income, thereby increasing the financial stability and well-being of those who pursue this kind of work.

Indeed, startups can come in all shapes and sizes, and may arise from a variety of motivations, including the desire to address a particular need in the market, pursue a personal passion or creative pursuit, or simply generate additional income. Regardless of the form they take, startups have the potential to offer significant benefits to individuals and communities.

David J. Teece, in his research on strategic management, underscores the interdependence of economic development and growth on enterprise performance, which in turn is reliant on entrepreneurship and effective management.

Entrepreneurship plays a pivotal role in stimulating economic growth, and in a competitive economy, management must increasingly adopt an entrepreneurial mindset. He has presented the Dynamic Capabilities framework, which describes companies as entities comprised of unique specialists, resources, and assets that are difficult to replicate by others. Teece suggests that these assets should be viewed as services that can be provided by the company, and should be evaluated in light of the constantly changing business environment. This framework advocates for an approach to business that emphasizes evolution through intentional design (53). Enterprises of this nature will persist in their function as a driving force for innovation in the economy, and furthermore, they offer a promising avenue for channeling individuals' creative energies in the right direction.

The involvement of robots in entrepreneurial endeavors, alongside human entrepreneurs, can be significant. This is due to the similarity between the principles of entrepreneurship and the process of machine learning. However, the nature of entrepreneurship is much more ruthless, as businesses must learn to operate effectively or face failure.

3.3.2. CREATIVE ECONOMY ROLE

The creative economy is a concept that refers to an economic system based on the production, distribution, and consumption of creative goods and services. In this context, individuals are free to participate in the general economy by utilizing their own energy and creativity to create and promote their own projects.The term "creative" encompasses not only the state of the art, but also any craft-related products and services, including entertainment and science.

In a society where people are not forced to work, the creative economy provides an opportunity for individuals to engage in work that is fulfilling and meaningful to them. They can use their own energy and resources to participate in this economy, either by creating their own projects or by collaborating with others to bring new ideas to life. By doing so, they can contribute to the overall economic growth of society while also enjoying the personal satisfaction that comes from pursuing their passions.

At first glance, it may seem that such economic activities are merely a form of leisure or play. However, it is important to recognize that these activities have the potential to become a significant part of the economy and may even have unexpected consequences.

Yevgeny Zamyatin's novel "We" features a plot in which three people are given a one-month break from work as an experiment. During this time, they wander around near their usual workplace and look inside with hunger. On the tenth day, they can no longer bear it and take each other's hands, walking into the water and submerging themselves deeper and deeper until the water ends their suffering (32). This plot is meant to illustrate how people can be unhappy without work, but it is important to note that Robosocialism, unlike the scenario depicted in the novel, does not aim to eliminate work entirely. Rather, the creative economy will be one of several options available to people.

In the creative economy, the focus is on pursuing one's passion and actively engaging in work, rather than striving for unlimited growth. This approach stands in contrast to the traditional capitalist model, where corporations are solely focused on maximizing profits and delivering constant growth to shareholders.

In a robosocialist economy, the creative economy would be just one aspect of a larger system that is designed to provide for the needs and well-being of all members of society. While economic growth may still be a consideration, it would not necessarily be a top priority for the creative economy part, and it would not come at the expense of social and environmental sustainability. Instead, the creative economy would be focused on producing meaningful and fulfilling work and providing access to cultural and artistic expression for all members of society.

3.3.3. GAMES AND ARTIFICIAL UNIVERSE

While an unconditional basic income would provide individuals with a safety net to support their basic needs in a robosocialist economy, it is important to recognize that the sudden loss of employment could have a significant impact on people's mental well-being.

For many individuals, their jobs provide not only income, but also a sense of purpose, structure, and social interaction. The sudden loss of these aspects of daily life could be jarring, leading to feelings of anxiety, depression, and isolation. Moreover, the availability of free time and disposable income could lead some individuals to engage in unhealthy behaviors as a means of coping with the significant changes to their way of life.

To mitigate these potential negative outcomes, it will be essential to provide individuals with the tools and support necessary to adapt to the changing economic landscape. This could include access to education and training opportunities to develop new skills and pursue their passions, as well as counseling and mental health services to address any issues related to the loss of employment. Ultimately, the success of a robosocialist economy will depend not only on its ability to provide individuals with economic security, but also on its ability to support their mental health and well-being. By taking a comprehensive approach to the transition to a new economic system, we can ensure that all members of society are able to thrive and lead fulfilling lives.

To achieve these goals, our society has been utilizing games and virtual reality for many years. In fact, in recent times, the Meta company has begun their own ambitious project of creating metaverses.

The term "metaverse" refers to a hypothetical future iteration of the internet, where users can interact with a fully immersive and shared virtual space. It is often described as a collective virtual shared space that is created by the convergence of physical reality, virtual reality, and augmented reality. In a metaverse, users can interact with each other and digital objects in a three-dimensional environment that simulates the physical world. The concept of a metaverse has gained popularity in recent years with the development of virtual and augmented reality technology.

It is important not to view games and artificial universes solely as channels for creative energy. These platforms provide us with the opportunity to expand beyond our conventional reality and engage in different types of communication and relationship building, including economic interactions in alternative dimensions.

David J. Chalmers calls a "reality plus" the idea that there may be more to reality than what we currently understand or experience. That virtual realities are genuine realities. He suggests that in addition to the physical reality we know and perceive through our senses, there may be a further reality that includes conscious experience and other non-physical phenomena. He suggests that this "reality plus" may include subjective experiences, mental states, and other aspects of consciousness that are not currently accounted for in our scientific understanding of the world.

Our mental states and subjective experiences could be influenced and even produced by simulations, it follows that these simulations must be considered real in some sense. David J. Chalmers believes that simulations are not just mere representations of reality, but are actually part of the reality we experience.

Chalmers suggests that the fact that we can be fooled by simulations, such as virtual reality or computer-generated graphics, shows that there is a deep connection between the world we perceive and the world that is simulated. In other words, simulations are not just a superficial representation of reality, but they are intertwined with our conscious experience and perception of reality.

Describing the "Human-Focused design", the author of "Actionable gamification. Beyond points, Badges, and Leaderboards" Yu-Kai Chou writes that: "My ultimate aim is to enable the widespread adoption of good gamification and human-focused design in all types of industries. I care deeply about creating a world that is sustainably more enjoyable and productive". According to Yu-Kai Chou, gamification is not just about adding game elements to a product or service, but about designing for human motivation and engagement.

In this context, human-focused design can be seen as an approach to design that prioritizes the user experience and motivation, rather than just the functional aspects of the product or service. This approach is based on the understanding that humans are driven by a variety of intrinsic and extrinsic motivations, and that effective design must take these factors into account to create engaging and satisfying experiences.

In contrast, function-focused design may prioritize technical efficiency and performance, without considering the user's experience or motivation. While this approach may be effective in certain contexts, it can lead to products and services that are difficult to use, frustrating, or unengaging. The investigations conducted by Yu-Kai Chou demonstrate that games serve as a means for us to experience reality, and are closely aligned with the concept of Reality+.

4. ROBO SOCIALISM ALTERNATIVES

4.1. ROBOFASCISM

As we consider the potential outcomes of the rise of automation and AI, it is important to acknowledge that there are various stakeholders involved, including governments, corporations, and society as a whole. However, it is possible that in certain scenarios, democratic governments and societies may become weakened, allowing corporations (fasces) to gain complete control over the development and implementation of automation tools and artificial intelligence. This could lead to a situation where the priorities of these corporations are solely focused on maximizing profit and efficiency, potentially disregarding the impact on society and the workforce. In such a scenario, corporations would likely focus primarily on developing and utilizing robots exclusively, leaving human labor owners in a very weak position. As corporations shift their priorities from human labor to robotic labor, the state of society could deteriorate.

According to Mussolini, the fascism is an anti-individualistic conception of "the guild or corporative system in which divergent interests are coordinated and harmonized in the unity of the State" (41). Despite the central role that the State and Nation play in fascist declarations and doctrines, in reality as we can see from the history of 20th Century, it often translates to a small number of wealthy clans or corporations forcibly occupying the political stage and claiming that 'the State is Us', leaving the rest of the populace fearful and working and dying in the interests of those corporations. This is because individuals are expected to sacrifice their lives for the sake of spiritual unity, while the leaders who promote this unity often enjoy the benefits of their position.

If robots are able to replace a significant amount or even all human labor, the value of human life may become even more insignificant for the fascist State. Rather than working and dying in the interests of the corporate State, people may find their role reduced to simply dying in the interests of the corporate State.

In the next step of the "Artificial Intelligence Revolution," corporations may also show interest in developing and deploying Mindroids, which are autonomous agents capable of replacing humans not only as workers but also as consumers. If such Mindroids work, they could get paid for their labor. This could further erode the role of human beings in the economy and society, as well as create new ethical and social challenges. Humans will become "second class" creatures and will be oppressed and forced to do everything that the fascists in power order them to do just to survive.

Robots based on AI technology have the potential to be more efficient and cost-effective than human workers, which may result in the displacement of human workers and human consumers. This could have significant consequences not only for the economy but also for the course of human history. Furthermore, if these robots are linked together and controlled by a massive AI network, that network may ultimately displace human workers and human corporations alike. This would result in a planet inhabited solely by artificial agents, governed by a giant all-encompassing AI. Such a scenario would fundamentally alter the nature of human existence and the very fabric of society.

The obvious recipe to prevent such a scenario could involve giving governments a representative role in the interests of all participants, not just corporations, and also ensuring government transparency and openness.

4.2. TECHNO TOTALITARIANISM

In an alternative scenario, if governments were to take more control over automation tools and AI, and if societies and corporations were unable to prevent it, then the state would have exclusive power to control individuals regardless of their status. This control would extend beyond mere surveillance and recognition of individuals for later blackmailing, to the ability to completely cut off people from their lives. This could be done through actions such as closing bank accounts, deleting all records related to property ownership, concealing identity and medical healthcare records, and more. Such a scenario would raise significant concerns over personal freedoms and privacy.

In such a scenario, the governmental machine would undoubtedly become a powerful weapon for domestic policy, allowing it to take control over the entire power structure of any country, block of countries, or even the entire world. The concentration of power in a single entity's hands would inevitably lead to authoritarianism and later to a totalitarian government because all sides of personal and public life could be physically controlled. "I do it because I am able to do it".

The ownership and control of technology can be likened to the control and ownership of ground resources, such as oil and gas. When a select few individuals or groups have control over such resources, it often leads to authoritarianism or even a totalitarian regime. Those in power tend to want to maintain their control and increase their power by concentrating the resources under their control. The same applies to automation, robots, and artificial intelligence - they are a valuable resource, like oil and gas, that can be controlled by a competitive group of individuals or used as a weapon against the majority of society.

This is precisely why the concept of robosocialism advocates against nationalizing automation and AI resources. Instead, it suggests transparently dispersing these resources while encouraging mutual usage. By doing so, the control and ownership of these technologies can be shared among a larger group of people, leading to more equitable distribution of power and resources. Ultimately, this could help prevent the rise of authoritarianism and totalitarianism that could arise from the concentration of power in the hands of a select few.

4.3. AUTOMATED COMMUNISM

Let us consider a more utopian scenario, where governments and large corporations relinquish their power and human labor owners - the people - assume control. In this scenario, the people collectively decide to make automation tools, artificial intelligence, and especially energy sources common property. This idea is reminiscent of the concept of 'Fully Automated Luxury Communism' put forth by Aaron Bastani. The term 'luxury' comes into play when the author defines that Wealth should be collective, and consequently, the quality of life for the entire society will become luxurious. "Communism is luxurious - or it isn't Communism".

In the Soviet Union, there existed a committee known as the State Planning Committee, or Gosplan for short. Its primary responsibility was to create and oversee a series of five-year plans that governed the economy of the USSR. In the planned economy of the USSR, the method of material balances was used as a tool for central economic planning. The Soviet government used this method to calculate the production targets and material requirements for various industries and enterprises throughout the country. Material balances were based on a detailed analysis of the inputs and outputs of production, and were used to determine the necessary quantities of raw materials, energy, and other resources needed to meet the production targets. The accuracy of material balances was critical to the success of the planned economy, as any miscalculation could lead to imbalances in the supply of materials, production disruptions, and inefficiencies. Therefore, material balances were closely monitored and adjusted over time to ensure that the economy was operating as efficiently as possible.

There were also investigations of Oscar Lange and Abba Lerner, which led to the development of the Lange-Lerner theorem. They have conducted an investigation into a simulation of supply and demand, similar to that of a capitalist economy, but in the context of central planning.

Lange Model (35) is a method for determining market-clearing prices in a socialist economy, where the government controls the production of goods. The model involves manufacturers producing goods until the price of a good is equal to its marginal cost, and then adjusting the price up or down based on whether there is a shortage or surplus of the product. This process continues until prices settle, resulting in market-clearing prices that are social welfare maximizing, which is a goal of socialism. Lange argued that capitalism cannot achieve truly social-welfare-maximizing prices because demand prices do not reflect the true needs of individuals due to unequal ownership of the means of production. Although the Lange Model has faced criticism, it remains relevant to discussions of socialist economics today and provides insight into how a socialist economy could be feasible.

In contrast to the time of the USSR and Gosplan, we now possess significantly greater computing power, advanced tools, and sophisticated algorithms. With these resources at our disposal, we can not only construct highly effective economy-wide planning models, but also take into account the needs and preferences of individuals. This is possible due to advancements in technology, which enable us to survey people's preferences and behaviors in real time.

On the other hand, as with any other centralized system, it bestows immense power to a small group of individuals and can swiftly lead to an authoritarian or totalitarian regime with dictatorship. Furthermore, if people have access to everything they desire, with no scarcity and everything up to luxury standards, they may lack motivation to continue striving. On the contrary, humans are wired to compete with one another, not only for survival necessities like food, but also for things like attracting mates and distinguishing themselves from others. Thus, while material luxury can provide social security, depriving people of private property can lead to a situation similar to that of the USSR, where private property is de facto simulated and egalitarian governmental officials have priority access to resources, leading to a potential demonstration of their "egalitarianism" through restricting access to others. Furthermore, if everything were controlled exclusively by AI, with no human input, it could be considered the greatest hazard to humanity as no individual would have any control over the system.

4.4. STARTUP PUNK UTOPIA

We cannot consider this scenario as a serious one, at least for now, and it is better to refer to it as a utopia. However, if we examine situations where one single component dominates, it is worth taking a closer look at the case. For instance, what would happen if entrepreneurs were to lead our community and dictate their interests to the people?

Dirk Helbing, in his discussion paper on Economics 2.0 or Socionomics, highlighted the possibility that some big and complex issues may become so overwhelming for humanity that they will need to be managed from the bottom-up. According to Helbing "a decentralized approach is an important precondition for success, while the implementation of homogeneous rules in large areas is expected to reduce diversity and innovation" (56). The author sees startups not just as limited to companies, but also encompassing political parties and other established institutions. In this view, people can come together and organize themselves in temporary projects around these institutions to achieve certain goals, before eventually terminating the project and forming new ones for achieving further objectives.

The idea of a startup utopia can be considered mostly as a utopia because startups face numerous challenges and limitations that make it difficult to achieve a perfect utopia. While startups are often associated with innovation, agility, and disruptive potential, they are also constrained by limited resources, competition, and a high risk of failure.

One of the biggest challenges faced by startups is their dependence on investors for funding. Startups typically have limited financial resources and rely heavily on venture capital firms, angel investors, and other sources of funding to finance their operations and growth. This dependence can lead to conflicts of interest and compromises in the pursuit of the startup's original vision and goals. Moreover, startups are often subject to market forces that are beyond their control, such as changing consumer preferences, disruptive technologies, and economic downturns. These external factors can derail even the most promising startups and make it difficult to achieve long-term success.

While startups may not have the resources to rule society, they can still be a viable means to drive the economy forward. As discussed in the chapter on "Startups and Entrepreneurship," startups are often viewed as a promising method for promoting innovation and solving various problems faced by large corporations, governments, and human societies.

Startups can provide a fresh perspective and approach to solving complex problems that have eluded traditional institutions. Their lean and agile nature allows them to quickly adapt to changes in the market and consumer preferences, making them more nimble and responsive than their larger counterparts. Additionally, startups can attract top talent, boosting economic growth and revitalizing local communities.

The notion of a society where startups are the means of optional earning seems plausible, particularly in a society where basic social security needs are met through automation benefits. In such a scenario, individuals could potentially dedicate their time and resources towards creating and growing startups, rather than solely focusing on entertaining. This type of society could foster a culture of entrepreneurship, where individuals are encouraged to pursue their own ideas and passions, and to take risks in order to achieve success.

4.5. HUMANS ANNIHILATION AND THE BIG REBOOT

If humanity chooses not to address the issue of powerful AI, and none of the scenarios discussed above take place, then the continued accumulation of problems related to capitalism could lead to a host of environmental, financial, and energy crises. These crises could result in widespread conflict and wars, as different nations and groups compete for limited resources. Additionally, the current level of technology in weaponry poses a significant threat to the survival of humanity, with the potential for catastrophic outcomes should a major conflict occur.

The consequences of failing to address the issue of powerful AI and the problems related to capitalism could be devastating, with the potential for humanity to be destroyed or reduced to a primitive state. The possibility of a "big reboot" scenario may exist, but it is more likely that such an outcome would occur without us.

Ultimately, we have a choice to make. We can continue down the path of unchecked capitalism and risk catastrophic outcomes, or we can take proactive measures to address these challenges and work towards a more sustainable and equitable future. The decision we make today will have a profound impact on the world we leave to future generations.

Потому что разум побеждает

REFERENCES

1. Karl Marx, Capital, Volume I. Chapter 15.1 "The development of machinery" page 492. Penguin Books, London 1990

2. David Ricardo, "On The Principles of Political Economy and Taxation". Chapter 31 "On machinery" https://www.marxists.org/reference/subject/economics/ricardo/tax/ch31.htm

3. Karl Marx, Capital, Volume I. Chapter 7.1 "The labour process" page 283-284. Penguin Books, London 1990

4. Veronika Semenova, Evgeny Petrichenko, "Information: The History of Notion, Its Present and Future". Izvestiya University. The North Caucasus Region, 2022 https://cyberleninka.ru/article/n/informatsiya-istoriya-ponyatiya-ego-nastoyaschee-i-buduschee

5. David Brion Davis, "The problem of Slavery in Western Culture". Page 72. Oxford 1966 https://books.google.de/books?id=lyodFB4SdOIC

6. MacKinsey Global Institute, 2017, https://www.mckinsey.com/featured-insights/future-of-work/jobs-lost-jobs-gained-what-the-future-of-work-will-mean-for-jobs-skills-and-wages

7. James Manyika, "Automation and the future of work", 2018 https://www.mckinsey.com/mgi/overview/in-the-news/automation-and-the-future-of-work

8. Leon Erlanger, "Computerworld", 2009. https://www.computerworld.com/article/2525995/the-tech-jobs-that-the-cloud-will-eliminate.html

9. Lewis Gersh, "The Velocity Of Obsolescence", Forbes, 2013. https://www.forbes.com/sites/lewisgersh/2013/07/29/the-velocity-of-obsolescence/?sh=594c6b3a6596
10. Karl Marx, "Capital. Volume I", p.274-275, Penguin classics, 1990, London.

11. Shoshana Zuboff, "The age of surveillance capitalism. The fight for a human future at the new frontier of power.", p. 376. Profile books, London, 2019.

12. Cathy O'Neil , "Weapons of Math Destruction: How Big Data Increases Inequality and Threatens Democracy", Location 140, Kindle Edition.

13. https://www.terraform.io

14. Paul Mason, "Postcapitalism. A guide to our future.", p. 175, Penguin books, 2016, UK

15. David J. Chalmers, "Reality+. Virtual worlds and the problems of philosophy", p. XVII, New York 2022.

16. Pamela Vachon, "How Much Cheaper Are Store-Brand Groceries Than Name Brands? We Do the Math", CNET, 2022. https://www.cnet.com/home/kitchen-and-household/how-much-cheaper-are-store-brand-groceries-than-name-brands-we-do-the-math/

17. Zachary Crockett, "Should we automate the CEO?", The Hustle, March 2023 https://thehustle.co/should-we-automate-the-ceo/

18. Tom Eisenmann, "Entrepreneurship: A Working Definition", Harvard Business Review, 2013, https://hbr.org/2013/01/what-is-entrepreneurship

19. David Graeber, "Bullshit jobs. The rise of pointless work and what we can do about it", p. 176-177. UK, 2018

20. Adam Smith, "The Wealth of Nations", p. 432. UK, 1999.
21. Tim Jackson, "Prosperity without growth. Foundations for the economy of tomorrow. Second edition", p. Amazon Poland, 2021

22. Frederick Herzberg, Bernard Mausner, Barbara Bloch Snyderman, "The Motivation to Work", https://books.google.de/books?id=KYhB-B6kfSMC

23. Sebastian Rödl, "Self-Consciousness and Objectivity: An Introduction to Absolute Idealism". 2018 https://books.google.de/books?id=8BhMDwAAQBAJ

24. Tim O'Reilly, "Was sollen wir von Künstlicher Intelligenz halten?", p. 197, Frankfurt am Main, 2017

25. George A. Bekey " Autonomous robots. From biological inspiration to implementation and control". https://www.google.com/books/edition/Autonomous_Robots/3xwfia2DpmoC

26. Bill Gates, "The Age of AI has begun", 2023, https://www.gatesnotes.com/The-Age-of-AI-Has-Begun

27. Archie B. Carroll, "Carroll's pyramid of CSR: taking another look", 2016, https://jcsr.springeropen.com/articles/10.1186/s40991-016-0004-6

28. Klaus Schwab, Peter Vanham, "Stakeholder Capitalism. A global economy that works for progress, people and planet", p. 56, New Jersey 2021

29. Klaus Schwab, Peter Vanham, "Stakeholder Capitalism. A global economy that works for progress, people and planet", p. 173, New Jersey 2021

30. Klaus Schwab, Peter Vanham, "Stakeholder Capitalism. A global economy that works for progress, people and planet", p. 225, New Jersey 2021
31. "Pause Giant AI Experiments: An Open Letter" March 2023, https://futureoflife.org/open-letter/pause-giant-ai-experiments/

32. Evgeniy Zamyatin, "We", Record Thirty-Four, 1924. Ebook Release Date: April 27, 2020 [EBook #61963] https://www.gutenberg.org/files/61963/61963-h/61963-h.htm

33. Karl Marx, Capital, Volume I. Chapter 15.6 "The compensation theory, with regard to the workers displaced by machinery" page 571. Penguin Books, London 1990

34. Aaron Bastani, "Fully Automated Luxury Communism", 2019 https://law.unimelb.edu.au/__data/assets/pdf_file/0009/3445353/2.-aaron-bastani-fully-automated-luxury-communism-a-manifesto-2.pdf

35. Cornell University, "The Lange Model of Socialism" https://blogs.cornell.edu/info2040/2015/10/19/the-lange-model-of-socialism/

36. Yu-Kai Chou, "Actionable gamification. Beyond points, Badges, and Leaderboards", p. Octalysis Media, 2014-2019, Amazon fulfillment, Wroclaw, Poland

37. Thomas Piketty, "Capital in Twenty-First Century", p. 609, Harvard University Press, 2017

38. Rutger Bregman, "Utopia For Realists and how we can get there", p. 31, 2018, Bloomsbury, London

39. Rutger Bregman, "Utopia For Realists and how we can get there", p. 32, 2018, Bloomsbury, London

40. "How many users does Facebook have?" https://www.oberlo.com/statistics/how-many-users-does-facebook-have
41. Benito Mussolini, "The Doctrine of Fascism", 1932, https://sjsu.edu/faculty/wooda/2B-HUM/Readings/The-Doctrine-of-Fascism.pdf

42. Joseph A. Schumpeter, "Capitalism, Socialism & Democracy", p. 132, London and New York, 2003

43. Joseph A. Schumpeter, "Capitalism, Socialism & Democracy", p. 83, London and New York, 2003

44. Thomas Piketty, "Capital in Twenty-First Century", p. 601-605, Harvard University Press, 2017

45. Dirk Riehle. "The Economic Case for Open Source Foundations." IEEE Computer, vol. 43, no. 1 (January 2010). Page 86-90. https://dirkriehle.com/publications/2010-selected/the-economic-case-for-open-source-foundations/

46. The Apache Software Foundation, https://www.apache.org

47. The Linux Foundation, https://www.linuxfoundation.org

48. The Linux Foundation Bylaws, https://www.linuxfoundation.org/legal/bylaws

49. *The Apache Software Foundation public records* *https://www.apache.org/foundation/records/*

50. *McKinsey report "The decoupling of GDP and energy growth: A CEO guide", 2019,* *https://www.mckinsey.com/industries/electric-power-and-natural-gas/our-insights/the-decoupling-of-gdp-and-energy-growth-a-ceo-guide*

51. *The World Bank, "GDP per unit of energy use", 1990-2015,* *https://data.worldbank.org/indicator/EG.GDP.PUSE.KO.PP.KD?end=2015&start=1990&view=chart*

52. *"World Energy Outlook 2022"* *https://www.iea.org/reports/world-energy-outlook-2022*

53. *David J. Teece, "Dynamic Capabilities & Strategic Management. Organizing for Innovation and Growth", 2009, Oxford, UK.*

54. *Nadia Eghbal, "Working in Public: The Making and Maintenance of Open Source Software", p. 43. 2020, California*

55. *Rossana Merola* International Labour Organization (ILO), Research Department, Geneva, Switzerland, Front. Artif. Intell., 31 May 2022 Sec. AI in Business Volume 5 - 2022* *https://www.frontiersin.org/articles/10.3389/frai.2022.867832/full*

56. *Dirk Helbing, "Economics 2.0: The Natural Step towards a Self-Regulating, Participatory Market Society", p. 28. 2013* *https://link.springer.com/article/10.14441/eier.D2013002*